...Barring Mechanicals

From London to Edinburgh and back,
on a recumbent bicycle

ANDY ALLSOPP

Cover design: Andy Allsopp
Set in Officina Sans 11.5/14pt
Typeset by Helen Hancox

ISBN 978-1-4452-5510-1

...Barring Mechanicals

From London to Edinburgh and back,
on a recumbent bicycle

ANDY ALLSOPP

To my darling wife, precious Evey.

Without you, I'd have neither strength nor opportunity to do this.

Nor the confidence to write it down.

You give me reason.

CONTENTS

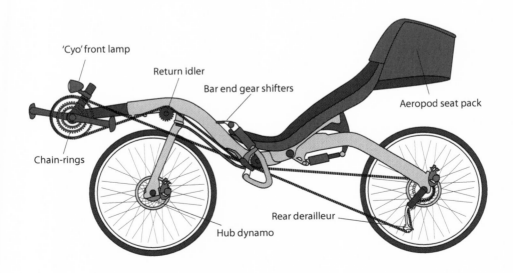

'Cyo' front lamp

Return idler

Bar end gear shifters

Aeropod seat pack

Chain-rings

Rear derailleur

Hub dynamo

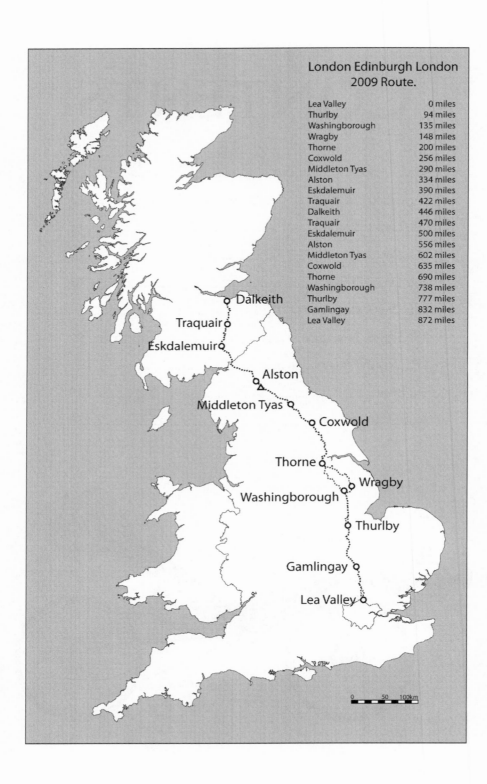

London Edinburgh London
2009 Route.

Lea Valley	0 miles
Thurlby	94 miles
Washingborough	135 miles
Wragby	148 miles
Thorne	200 miles
Coxwold	256 miles
Middleton Tyas	290 miles
Alston	334 miles
Eskdalemuir	390 miles
Traquair	422 miles
Dalkeith	446 miles
Traquair	470 miles
Eskdalemuir	500 miles
Alston	556 miles
Middleton Tyas	602 miles
Coxwold	635 miles
Thorne	690 miles
Washingborough	738 miles
Thurlby	777 miles
Gamlingay	832 miles
Lea Valley	872 miles

Dalkeith

Traquair

Eskdalemuir

Alston

Middleton Tyas

Coxwold

Thorne

Wragby

Washingborough

Thurlby

Gamlingay

Lea Valley

0   50   100km

FOREWORD

I'd like to share a little of how my LEL[1] came to be, because when I first started I was in awe of long distance cyclists. I was very aware of the differences between 'them' and 'me', but failed to see that the distinction was made on my side only...

At time of writing I'm 35 and my wife and 22-month-old boy are the centre of my world. Constantly butting against them are the demands of work. Between the two (quite literally) are 90% of my rides. I cyclo-commute when possible. I ride recreationally with friends. I am not a 'serious' cyclist.

Just after the birth of my son in early 2008 I was diagnosed with a degenerative spinal condition. When he was three months old I was pulled into hospital with a chance to correct it. Things went well and after only a few days I was learning to walk again. At my post-op consultation the surgeon explained that through careful physiotherapy and the passage of time I would regain use of my back, but would not be able to ride a bicycle again.

Fortunately, in addition to pessimists, the hospital also featured a wi-fi internet connection. It took me about three days to find a suitable bike builder online, spec' my first recumbent[2], then drag the laptop from room to room until medical opinion could be generally reversed. Orders were placed. Wives were appeased. Things began to look sparkly again.

By June I was pretty much mobile again. Walking progressed to wobbling around on the 'bent. In August I kicked off a four day mini tour of Normandy with a bunch of mates I've known since school. It all went very well. The 'bent (an HPV SMGTe) proved a supremely capable tourer, doing double shifts on luggage and tackling long days without any pain or complaint.

To celebrate, two of our number decided to set ourselves a bigger challenge. In November 2008 we signed up for LEL. I was averaging 10 miles a week.

---

1   *LEL is an audax of approximately 1400km, routing cyclists from London to Edinburgh and back, with a maximum time limit of 116hrs, 40 minutes. An audax (pronounced ow-dacks) is a non-competitive long-distance cycling event, following a designated but unmarked route through check points (controls) within specified time limits. Audax events are also known as randonnées.*

2   *A bicycle that places the rider in a laid-back reclining position. The rider typically travels feet first, with the pedals just below their eyeline. Unlike traditional diamond frame (DF) bicycles, 'bents can be rear or front wheel drive (RWD, FWD)*

The following month, my company relocated to an office in Chiswick, affording me a 33 mile round trip commute from Kent, directly over one of the steepest hills in the area. Three days a week, rain, shine or snow, I pedalled up to the TV mast and down to the river. There were plans for long(er) rides, but through the close of the year our prep was mostly office based: plugging average speeds into spreadsheets; making day plans; reading cycle forums; getting the hang of telling colleagues that I am planning to ride from London to Edinburgh and back; trying not to get freaked out when met with yet another blank stare...

The new year brought the first of our proper training rides. First 30 miles in one hit, then, a week later, a full 40 mile day. Through the cold snap of February 2009 I proudly raised my average speed to 12.8mph.

When the winter finally retreated we geared up for our first 50 miler. Unfortunately, the winter had been particularly unkind to the roads. My buddy's wheel found a pothole, earning us an early abandon and him a broken wrist.

With eight weeks in plaster before he could resume training, his LEL was clearly out. Neither of us had ridden an audax before and suddenly it looked like I'd be riding on my own. That March I put out a call for any training buddies in the area. Anyone vaguely local who wouldn't mind spending a day in the saddle.

Two riders from cyclechat.co.uk answered the call. One (Dellzeqq) was intimidatingly accomplished, taking me for a 'quick spin' and showing me that I could raise my average to 15mph over 62 miles. The only notable side effect was that the exertion near killed me. The other was (bless him) an almost complete newbie, heaps of ambition, 17 years old, shiny new bike. Went by the name of ilovebikes. ILB for short.

March brought significant events.

I spent another day in the company of Dellzeqq, gaining introduction to his friends Jurek of YACF[3] and Dave. We covered 104 miles in that sitting, riding out from London to Sandwich. On the way down, Dellzeqq recommended Dave and I a place on something called the FNRttC[4]. This proved to be an excellent idea. A chance to test my ability to ride greater distances, overnight, whilst tired, in near absolute safety.

---

3   *"yet another cycling forum"*

4   *The Friday Night Ride to the Coast is 60 mile social ride, leaving Hyde Park Corner at midnight under the full moon from March to November.*

Second, ILB suggested the ideal post-ride celebration for our first 65 mile FNRttC would be to ride back. It would be his virgin 100 and by the time we got home (130 miles) would be the furthest either of us had ridden in a single day.

Third, being vastly out of our depth, we cemented some fantastic friendships with other forumites on the ride back from the coast. Brian seemed to know every backroad between Brighton and London (provided it had a hill on it), Martin provided encouragement when spirits were flagging, Dave reappeared to keep excellent pace and provide a photographic record of our exploits. We leant heavily on them and they carried us admirably. If I recall correctly, Dave had bagged his virgin 100 only a few weeks prior, and it was Martin's first FNRttC. It never showed.

Lastly, I was forced to acknowledge that whilst the SMGTe had bullet-proof construction, extreme comfort and perfect stability, the 13kg weight penalty over my upright was having a noticeable effect on my ability to climb. Loaded up for the five day LEL, some of the hills would test the (already low) gearing.

David at Laid Back Bikes of Edinburgh came to the rescue, supplying me with a new Challenge Furai SL-II. We worked together on the spec', keeping the USS steering from the SMGTe, employing the same dynamo lighting and shedding 8 kgs of over-engineered German aluminium.

April came around and the training calendar began to really kick in. I claimed a pass from my wife to join the CycleChat 'tour of Hampshire' ride. This was my first time out on the Furai and suddenly I found I could compete with uprights. I logged 174 miles that day, 90% with other forumites, 10% in the small hours on my own.

Two weeks later, ILB and I took in a 73 mile loop to visit a (not so local) bikeshop in the pouring rain. I was getting the hang of longer distances and adverse weather. In the last week of April, I rode a second CycleChat excursion to Essex with the Bromley cyclists. 125 miles that day. 3 months 'til LEL. Looking good.

By May, our group had begun to formalise into 'The Mouseketeers'. Martin, Dave, ILB and I were becoming known for our inclination to ride to and from socials, logging enormous mileages on vastly unsuitable roads. Our enthusiasm for distance far outweighed our talent with maps and at least a third of our miles were generally in the wrong direction.

We proved the point on the CycleChat ride of the 2nd May. What we'd anticipated as a day's outing became a 231 mile excursion around Essex, earning me a trip to IKEA and a cycling ban on weekends.

Limited to commutes and one sneaky early morning ride (0500hrs, 72 miles) I finally got a reprieve at month's end and celebrated by spinning down to Bournemouth with ILB. Bit off a little more than we could chew and the remaining Mouseketeers sent out a rescue party to meet us at Stonehenge. The company lifted our spirits but we were forced to bail after 219 miles through sheer exhaustion.

The first weekend in June saw my second FNRttC (to Whitstable and back at 143 miles), swiftly tailed by another cycling ban. Damn. Overcooked it... Time to sit down and work out the boundaries.

Even with a young toddler in tow, Evey is inherently supportive of my 'needs'. She conceded to one more ride before LEL, on a weekend of her choosing. Fair on.

As our last chance to bag the elusive 400k, ILB and I targeted Dunwich (and back) on Sunday 28th June. I logged 257 miles that day and was still ok to cycle-commute the following morning.

Come July, I was out of time. Officially tapering for the event, I rode only commuting miles. Four months of preparation had bagged me eleven 'long' rides, all over 100kms, five over 100 miles and a final three over 200 miles. Most were at social pace, but even my commute was now averaging 15mph.

With one day to go, I was standing in the registration queue at Lea Valley Youth Hostel, trying to resist weighing my prospects against the other entrants. From what I'd heard of audaxing, there seemed to be a remarkable absence of the anticipated staples. Where were the bearded septuagenarians? Bring forth steel-framers with mudguards! Where I was looking for home made map holders, I found time trial styled aero bars with custom mounts for Garmins, all atop carbon framed steeds. The national kit of 30 countries seemed to be present, and the Italians were travelling everywhere in a peloton. Even on foot.

The magnitude of what I'd signed on for was suddenly kicking in. I blocked out the chatter of 600+ riders, returning home registered, a little afraid, and extremely excitable. I hadn't got all the training miles I'd hoped for, but my confidence was high. Grim determination would be enough. No reason I shouldn't make it round. ...Barring mechanicals.

Andy Allsopp
December 2009

26th Oct 2008, 14:56

arallsopp
Junior Member

Join Date: Aug 2008
Location: Bromley,
SE London
Posts: 51

LEL - Training advice

OK.

Humour me for a second. My long time cycling buddy has just asked if I want to join him in the LEL next year. The wife has said go for it. Work will give me the time off.

So, the only real obstacle is that this would be my (and his) first Audax, and that neither of us has ever ridden more than 110 miles in a day. I'm on an SMGTe, he's on a Marin San Anselmo. We both currently ride around 10 miles per week, so its quite a ramp up.....

So... anyone got any idea about how to make this a reality without it killing either of us? We've got 272 days to go I guess, which is longer than I had to train for the marathon, and that seemed to work...

Andy.

edit   quote

LEL Day 1: Sunday

London Edinburgh London
2009 Route.

Sunday

Lea Valley	0 miles
Thurlby	94 miles
Washingborough	135 miles

A Late Start

1030hrs Sunday morning, and I'm loading the bike onto the roof of a friend's car. He's agreed to whizz me around the M25 to the kickoff at Lea Valley, Cheshunt. My wife Evey, our son Teddy and the in-laws follow in our car (which is roomy enough for the 'bent and us, but not with the extended family along for the ride). This bit goes like clockwork. 1300hrs I arrive at Cheshunt and refuse to be utterly freaked out by the national teams present. The Greeks look friendly. The Italians have an entourage of support vehicles and mechanics. The Dutch are mostly horizontal. Excellent. The field of around 600 riders will set off in two tranches, one centred around 8am, the second at 2pm. I'm due to set off around 1415hrs, so there's plenty of time to play with Ted, try to relax, have a worry wee, etc.

I spend a few happy minutes wandering around Lea Valley, checking out kit. I'm keeping an eye out for people I might know who are on the ride. GerryC is one, whom I met on the FNRttCs. No sign. I do find a 'bent with a YACF Buff[5] aboard, and a little detective work in their forums soon puts a name to Rich Forrest. Looks like Gerry set off in the 0800 slot. Oh well, I'll join Rich when my time comes. Lovely.

Fast forward 10 minutes. I'm in the loos and I hear the 'clack clack' of a cleated rider on tile enter behind me (fnarr if you must). That's odd... Why am I not making the same noise? Look down. TRAINERS! Sh1t. Bad bad bad. Right. Exit loo. Find family. Explain.

---

5   *Lightweight multifunction headwear favoured by cyclists, falling somewhere between a scarf, snood and hat.*

1330hrs, and I'm holding the baby, entertaining the in-laws and watching buddy and wife plough through a cloud of dust and tyre smoke. The repmobile surges forwards in a manner entirely unlike a big grey Honda and, once the gravel settles, has gone.

45 minutes to get to Bromley and back. Hmmm... Took us an hour and a half to get here. This may not be an auspicious kick off. I wander over to the official start with Ted and watch massed groups set off in 15 minute intervals. After 1400hrs, each group gets considerably smaller. By 1440hrs, it's just me, a group of Catalans who outnumber their bikes, and (belatedly) a long-haired scouser who seemed to think the massed ride would set off at 3. I take some confidence in this. At least I knew what time I was supposed to leave, even if I'm running late.

I look up to see an indiscriminate family saloon get airborne on the level crossing, maintain speed whilst turning into the station car park balanced solely on the driver's side front wheel, brake late and fling open the doors. I'm expecting Starsky and Hutch, or at least Mssrs Clarkson and Hammond, but the first figure I pull out of redshift is my wife. In her hand, my shoes. This is suddenly looking better.

Their arrival garners a round of applause from the remaining onlookers (cyclists cheer a car for erratic driving? Got to be a first!) and I grab the shoes, point the 'bent at the starting line, collect the aforementioned LongHairedScouser and set off.

At The Start Line
Photo: Mr Larrington

Sunday 1445hrs
Miles ridden: 0. Your time starts NOW.

OK. Off the line. LongHairedScouser in tow, GPS[6] working lovely, a few too many speedhumps for my choice of route, but it's drawing me out of town and towards Edinburgh. Suburbia drops somewhere behind us and the countryside steps in to welcome us aboard. Every time I glance at the GPS I see we're moving at 16+mph. The sun is shining. This is good. LongHairedScouser and I are in pleasant conversation about navigation (he admits to being utterly lost already and is happy/requiring to follow me and the GPS to the first control).

Now, a quick word about recumbents. They're very comfortable. They can be very fast. They *all* have issues with chain management. In the rear wheel drive Furai this role is supplied by a set of jockey wheels routing the chain line up and down, following the frame. One in particular (the foremost return idler) has the delightful job of keeping the chain out of the front wheel.

So, 9.4 miles in, and my eye catches a wobble in the guide fixed to the foremost return idler. I can stop and sort that. Tiny bit of plastic. Probably just worked loose.

PING! Sh1t! It's come off.

CRACK!! ...and gone straight under a car. That's bad. OK, jockey wheel still there. Never seen the chain mount the guide. Probably just there for aesthetics. Still, let's stop and check.

---

6   *Global Positioning System, a satellite-based navigation system using transmitted signals and mathematical triangulation to pinpoint location. Consumer models are normally hand-held and battery operated, and may include additional information to support routing, terrain, elevation, speed and more.*

PING! Sh1t. That was a retaining guide then. Jockey wheel gone now. Doing 20mph. Best throw on the anchors.

SCHLLINGGG! Cr@p! chain is in the front wheel. Can't steer. Can't pedal. Unclip. Get ready for crash landing.

SKKKCRRRANK! [Chain catches spoke and brings rider and 'bent to a very rapid halt]. Stop. Breathe. Relax. OK. You're alive. That was bad. Am I in traffic? No. OK. Good. Where's my LongHairedScouser? Up ahead. Looping back. OK. Good.

Let's check bike over. Hmmm... In place of jockey wheel and two retaining guides, I seem to have a bare spindle. Damn. Can I balance the chain on it? No. Damn. Try again. Damn. No. OK. Can I fix this? Erm. No.

10 minutes pass, whilst the LongHairedScouser and I try to work out where on the route sheet[7] we actually are. I momentarily consider loaning him my GPS, as it looks like I'm out of the running. Damn. On second thoughts, I'll need it to find a station. Sh1t. Not happy. Best ring wife and buddy. See if anyone is still in the area, or whether I'm lugging this thing back on the trains.

---

7   *A list of the turn instructions for an audax event. Often provided in summary form, route sheets use abbreviations for both directions and junctions: L = left; R = right; SO = straight over; T = T junction; TL = traffic light; O = roundabout; X = Crossroads*

Sunday 1522hrs
Miles ridden: 9.5. Walking to the station.

OK. Well I seem to be in Hertford. That sounds like it'll have a station. Wonder what their Sunday service is like. Best go find out. GPS guides me to Railway Street. I sit kerbside and post an update to various forums. 'Buzz!' goes the Blackberry. A reply has been posted to a topic you are watching... the text of the reply is shown below.

"If you have some big zip-ties [I ask tentatively!] you might be able to bodge a workaround – just make a loop for the chain to pass through. Might be a bit noisy and you might have to replace the ties every now and then, but it could get you on your way."

No. That won't work. Will it? I've got 10 in my bag. Worth a punt. 9 yards later SCHLLINNNK BANG. OK. No. Hmmm.. Cut it loose. Try again. One zip-tie over the spindle. Another zip-tie around the frame. Back pedal. Hideous noise. Lift the rear and try forwards. Seems to work. Catches on the power links, but otherwise good. Retrace my steps. Get back to the route. Check the ties. Hmmm. Chain is slowly sawing through. Hope to hell there's someone who's set off behind me who happens to have more zip-ties.

Ties in the bag: 7.

Sunday 2200hrs
Miles ridden: 79. Miles walked: 6.
Stolen materials.

OK. My apologies to the owner of the lost cat in Upton. Your sign may not be as neatly retained as it once was.

On the plus side, I'm now rolling again. Ran out of zip-ties about 8 instructions back. Its raining. Deep suspicion that I've managed to miss the optional stop at Gamlingay, and now fair worried that I'll be out of time for the next one. I daren't look at the clock. Sun is down. Can't be more than ten miles from here to the checkpoint. Maybe I'm still in the game. Come on baby, hold together... The ground has levelled out now. Six hours in the rain hasn't dampened my spirits (yet). My dynamo lights were less interested by a pedestrian pace, so the new tie is very welcome. Walking darkened lanes has given me plenty of time to mentally review the task in hand.

From my office prep when the year was young, I'm pretty sure Thurlby closes at 20:35hrs. I guess I set off a little late, but I'm not sure this is going to wash with the officials. Thurlby is a mandatory check point, so if I don't show my face there before the cut, I get a DNF[8]. Until I ran out of ties, I was doing 20mph sprints for five mile blocks. I daren't push too hard on the last tie. Its been dark for a while. An oncoming estate car flashes its lights as it passes me, swings round in my rear view mirror, pulls alongside momentarily, then sits in front at 17mph. The cat's owner? Damn. This bike is conspicuous. No. Worse. The sag wagon.

Not now. Surely. I was almost there.

---

8   *'Did Not Finish'*

Well I'm not stopping without hitting at least one control, even if it's closed. Exhausted, I follow it. Two miles later, red tail lights turn off the main road, down a high street, into a side lane, onto a car park. Looks like this is where it ends.

Sunday 2244hrs
Miles ridden: 88. Miles walked: 6.
Arrive Thurlby Primary School.

"Howdo. Sorry I'm late. Are you still open?"

"Oh yes. We're not shutting for a good few hours yet. 544 right? You're the last in. Give us your brevet card[9] and I'll get you stamped."

"Stamped? I thought the last stamp was half eight?"

"It is, if you set off at 8am."

"...."

Big smiles. Note to self. Remember brain stops working when sugar is low. OK. I have almost four hours in the bag. This is far from the plan, but it's workable. I'm very wet. I'm very hungry. I'm going to lose a lot of speed once the going gets hilly, so it's imperative that I don't give back any of the spare I've just bagged. I'm figuring it's flat(ish) from here to Middleton Tyas, but then I've got a very nasty six in a row of Alston, Eskdalemuir, Dalkeith, Eskdalemuir and Alston again. That's Cumbria, Northumberland, Scottish Borders, Midlothian and back, and is going to cost me considerably. Must not stop here any longer than necessary.

Right. Grab a warm drink and a plate of food. Thaw out the brain, then set off. ASAP.

This works. The volunteers manning the control are excellent, service is top notch (well, I am pretty much the only rider there), and I'm even beginning to dry out. 14 minutes after arriving I'm feeling human, am back out the door, am looking for my bike.

---

9   Audax riders carry a brevet card, onto which information is added at each control as proof that the route was followed.

An entirely unexpected tech interrupts my search to say "I've fixed her up as best as I can. Bunged a new tie around the axle. Couldn't find a jockey wheel or replacement part, so I've fashioned this, out of a cleat back."

Under torchlight, I see the old spindle, now cased in fresh zip-ties, with a suitably low-tech protuberance bolted onto the side. The chain sits snugly on the ball race, with the frame blocking its exit left, and the cleat back right. Blimey. It's ugly. But it holds.

We spend 10 minutes refining the positioning and as the food kicks in I suddenly feel full of confidence. The road onward is dark and remote, but the next check point is only 40 odd miles north of here. I can be there by 2am. In a tradition continued by volunteers at every control from here on in, he gives me a bag of ties and waves me on.

Sunday 2311hrs
On through the night

Right. Next up, Washingborough. Set the GPS, get a lock and go. Lound, Edenham, Elsthorpe, Bulby, flat lands stretch out in front. Steadily northwards. Kirkby Underwood, Aslackby, Sleaford. Long straight roads. Never realised there was so much countryside left.

Navigating on an Audax is an odd experience. In many ways you're utterly integrated into the environment. It's dark. You're dark. It rains. You get wet. Birds call as you approach. Rabbits scurry in your wake. There's nothing between you and them. 'Them' is grass, animals, families, trees, clouds, gravel, hedges, white lines, tarmac. It's immersive, more like swimming through a photo album than sitting atop a bike.

In another part of your head, your brain is actively stripping all this redundant data away, to better compress the journey into a handful of turn instructions. If you're the kind that panics about missing turnings (I am), you come to appreciate those that offer additional information. L is tough. L:T (T being T-Junction) will resolve itself when you run out of road. L:TL (traffic lights) you'll even see coming.

Somewhere the wrong side of 1am, I've just left the village of Ruskington behind me, and the next instruction (R:TL) isn't for 12 miles. Digby, or Branston, perhaps. The rain has let up. The road is straight and flat. I'm not likely to miss a set of traffic lights, so this is a good chance to get some real speed underway.

The tarmac resolves to a low hum, cranks spin, the wind drowns the complaints from my rattling chain. After what seems like only a few minutes, I can already pull out the red filters on the junction ahead. Making good progress. 10 minutes later and I'm seemingly no closer. Through Digby, but the lights are still way up the road. I'm more tired than I thought. Can't seem to close the gap. 20 minutes later, and I see both lamps suddenly swing right. A moment of revelation. Cyclists!

I've found the back of the pack. Minutes later, I roll into the Washingborough checkpoint. There's a tech on the gate, and he's got a bag of zip-ties.

"I read your post!"

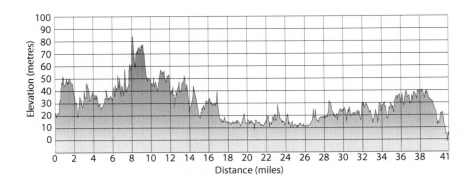

LEL Day 2: Monday

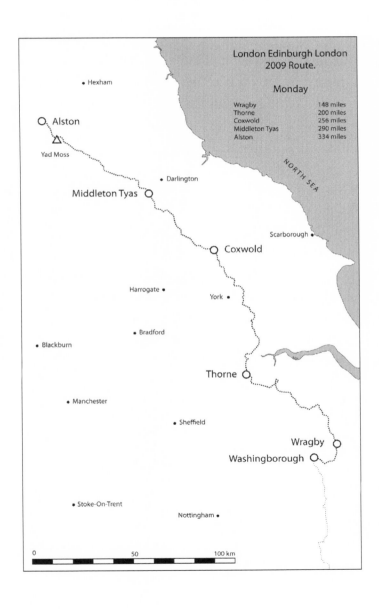

London Edinburgh London 2009 Route.

Monday

Wragby	148 miles
Thorne	200 miles
Coxwold	256 miles
Middleton Tyas	290 miles
Alston	334 miles

NORTH SEA

Hexham

Alston

Yad Moss

Darlington

Middleton Tyas

Scarborough

Coxwold

Harrogate

York

Bradford

Blackburn

Thorne

Manchester

Sheffield

Wragby

Washingborough

Stoke-On-Trent

Nottingham

0   50   100 km

Monday 0151hrs
Arrive Washingborough. Miles travelled: 135.

Feeling good. The tough stuff is momentarily out of the way. Aboard a recumbent, I knew I'd be riding some of the sections on my own, but I hadn't prepared for 130 odd miles without sight or sign of another rider. It feels good to be in a room with other cyclists. Hard to be downbeat surrounded by spandex. My new found confidence tempts me to stop and sleep a while. I'm 19 hours into my day, but I'm well settled in my routine. The bike is behaving and I still have a handful of ties in the bag from Thurlby. I've refined their application, and am getting up to 20 miles out of each now. At this rate, I'll end up in profit.

I review the brevet card and see that the next checkpoint is pretty close. The minimum pace dictates that I keep an average of 7.5mph, *including* any time spent off the bike eating, resting, sleeping, et al. Already I can sense that the needs of the soul are going to need careful balance against biology. With the visible lift I'm getting from the surrounding randonneurs[10], I know there's no way I can do this alone. These are the backmarkers though. People who suffered technical problems, routing mishaps. Much as I hate to leave their camaraderie, I've got to head on.

---

10 *A participant in a randonnée or audax*

Monday 0225hrs
Into the darkness.

Nice flat run out through Booths Branston and Potterhanworth. The ground has dried up. Only a few hours ago I was convinced I'd been routed through a ford. Now the sky is clear, the air is light. There may even be a tailwind. I begin to see blinkies up front again.

Over the river and through Bardney. The road begins to snake left and right around fields, each turn reveals another set of lamps to chase. I'm slowly moving into the pack. It's beginning to feel like a FNRttC.

Through Kingthorpe and I see the unmistakable altitude of a recumbent tail-light upfront. I chase it down to find an American on what looks like a front faired Rans. Nice bike. Fields give way to houses. Streetlamps spring up. I'm three instructions from Washingborough, in Wragby, and the control is upon me.

Monday 0315hrs
Arrive Wragby. Miles travelled: 148.
Time elapsed: 12.5 hours.

Either I'm speeding up, or that was a very short leg. The Rans arrives a few minutes behind me. Our control is positioned under traffic lights and is recognisable by a few stationary cyclists, a parked car, a phonebox and a motor home alleged to be full of snoozing Italians.

I'm definitely catching the field. No time (or place) to stop here though, and the next checkpoint is 50+ miles north. I glean a few minutes' conversation, get my brevet car stamped, water the wall and set off again. The plan is resolving towards riding through the bulk of 24 hours before sleep.

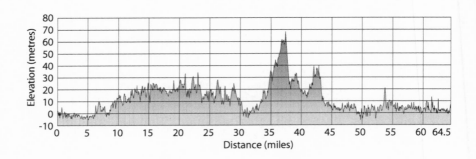

Monday 0322hrs
Meet the pack.

Wragby drops behind me, long straight roads continue. Instructions are few and far between. I chase down more cyclists as the road traces around field boundaries between Holton cum Beckering, Lissington, Middle Rasen, Osgodby, Kirkby. I'm starting to pick out hills on my right, but the road up ahead looks as flat as Bb minor. Oswersby South and North drop away. I'm running out of country to the east, and the route responds by flirting at the border of North Lincolnshire with tentative stabs alternately west and southward. I stay west through Thorton le Moor, South Kelsey and Waddingham before finally slipping across the border a few miles outside Kirton Lindsey.

From here the land seems to get a little hillier. It's only gentle rollers, though, and I continue north-west inland, presumably routing for a narrow point on the Humber. Messingham brings a sunrise and a nice downhill stretch with a long run off. I take the chance to claim a few more blinkies before they're switched off.

Just before 6am I hit a big river at East Butterwick and am surprised to find it's the Trent. To me, this means Nottingham, but in my addled state I can't work out if I'm north or south of it (45 miles north, it later transpires). I'm surprised to find myself keeping pace with a homebrew FWD[11] recumbent I'd spotted at Lea Valley. Enormous front ring and square-section tubing, this is a serious piece of kit. The German at the helm probably weighs less than it does, but at the rate it's rusting my guess is they'll even out somewhere around Alston. Adding insult to (very probable) injury, he seems to have brought a suitcase on the rear rack. He's fast though. As traffic builds, he drops

---

11   Unlike traditional diamond frame (DF) bicycles, 'bents can be rear or front wheel
      drive (RWD, FWD)

in front with ease before swinging back to continue our conversation. He rides calmly, one hand on the bars, the other snapping me with a handheld camera. Given that we're rolling at 16mph all the way, I'm guessing he's been able to convert some of the slack he must have earned into sleep.

Approaching Gunness
(Photo: Joachim Janssen)

I stay with him along the East bank up to the bridge at Gunness, where we clamber back south through 'thorpes Al and Derry. Entering Beltoft I am very grateful to my wife for reading through the routesheet with me on the Saturday night. As each town comes up, I can hear her voice counting off its name. Continue east through Belton, Westgate, into South Yorkshire. Schoolboy geography tells me to expect hills, but there's even a canal here. The German and I cross it together and roll into the rugby club on the edge of Thorne.

Monday 0708hrs
Miles travelled: 200. Arrive Thorne.

Down a little concrete ramp, round the corner and the first thing I notice is that there are *lots* of bikes here. Some look seriously fast. Admittedly, their owners may have been indoors getting 8+hours kip by the time I rolled in, but I now definitely feel part of the gang again.

I go inside to grab some food and a hot drink. As suspected, the room is full of dormant randonneurs. Entirely unexpectedly, 90+% of them are simply lying on the floor. Maybe ten have blankets. The rest look like ruined statues, heroic legs broken, lying wherever they fell.

I freshen the zip-ties on the 'bent, grab some food, then start looking for a 2ft x 6ft section of floor that I can reach. I've been up for over 24 hours now and am starting to lose focus. Sleep is clearly going to be of varying quality, and with the brightness outside (and in) I know that I can't waste too much sunlight simply lying down. I roll up my spare jersey, pull the buff over my face, set my phone alarm for 90 minutes and curl up around it like a baby.

The noise slowly fades and I'm long gone by the time someone takes the opportunity to snap me.

Asleep at Thorne, Northbound
Photo: Greg Melia

Just after nine I wake up. Breakfast is a welcome, but bewildering, process. Body and mind are still unsure why we aren't still asleep. You know the feeling of walking out of a cinema into sunlight? It's like that, but the sunlight is fluorescent tubes. Nothing is quite real and everything is just slightly green.

Stomach is kick-started when breakfast lands and sends the fuel out in search parties to look for a brain. My eyes are drawn to a rider across the room. Something about his jersey. Retro, or bargain? I've seen it before. Looks like Brian from my first FNRttC. Can't be sure until I see his bike. No recognition in his eyes as yet. I approach. No. It *is* him. Major confidence boost. I finish my coffee in happy conversation.

Monday 0955hrs
Minutes slept: 90. North again.

Brian leaves in a small group about six minutes ahead of me. I give chase through Moorends and catch them midway through the Dutch landscape into Rawcliffe. Curiosities of the FNRttC mean that I have only ever spoken with Brian when I haven't had enough sleep. Today will integrate nicely.

We ride side by side for a while – Brian, his mate, and me. Brian takes exception on crossing a second canal (the Knottingley and Goole at Rawcliffe Bridge) and begins to rant at the lack of hills. This is classic Brian really. I sympathise, but have no empathy at all. In my book, hills are A Bad Thing™. Brian is right though. As we skirt along the River Aire, then over the Ouse, even I will admit that it's hard to get a sense of progress when the landscape refuses to offer anything other than a horizon.

On through Howden, Highfield (presumably ironically named, as it's at the same elevation as everything else within 50 miles), Sutton-upon-Derwent, Elvington. We skirt anticlockwise around York, five miles out, to the south-east, then due north. I pass places I visited with my school when I was 14. Seems very strange to be here on a pushbike. On the way out we are rewarded with a few bumps, which Brian tears into with enthusiasm.

It's just after midday and the sun is out in force. Layers are removed and the group separates. As I pass Strensall Camp, I begin to detect serious hills up front. We alternate north and east around long shallow hedges, but there is no doubt they are getting closer. Exiting Stillington, one in particular looms up in front. Given the relative level of its immediate environs, it looks for all the world like the fields are a patchwork quilt laid over a bed, only someone's left an umbrella stand on top of the mattress. The next instruction on the route sheet sends us directly towards it.

I'm looking at the GPS, which is telling me I need to make an L in 1.3 miles. I can see a suitable turning just before the bottom of the hill and I'm desperately trying to gauge the distance. Looks about right though, and I ride on watching the "distance to next" slowly count down. Too close to call. We're either going around or straight over the top. The miles tick away very slowly. A mile later, I reach the outskirts of Crayke and the bottom of the hill.

I swing left out of blind hope, but the GPS bleeps at me until I give in and loop back. I pitch myself up, and when I do finally reach the L, find the road climbs even higher behind the houses. After a morning of being between 0 and 20m above sea level, 140m all at once is quite a hit.

I take my reward in the undulations following the descent, but climbing into Oulston I can see it's going to be pretty bad from here on in. One final descent drops me from Newburgh Grange to Coxwold and I arrive at the control full of smiles.

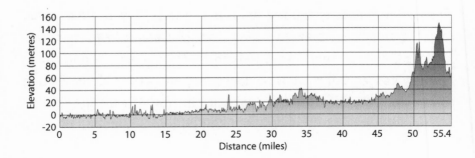

Monday 1336hrs
Miles travelled: 256. Arrive Coxwold.
Unnecessary and enormous hills traversed: 1.

This is good. It's a beautiful day and cyclists are milling around the car park enjoying the warm sun on their skin and some time off the bikes. I spy Rich Forrest's 'bent and head indoors to look for him. At the queue for food I recognise Brian's shirt once more.

"Suppose you think that was funny, Brian?"

"Bit steep, neh? Nice to have something to push against for a while though."

The man clearly has issues.

I find Rich and am saddened to hear he's unable to continue. Shorts had gone renegade and were attacking him all the way from Washingborough. Complexion of raw bacon in places you really don't want it. Nearest sensible bail is his brother's place at Wetherby so he's still 30+ miles from comfort. I lighten his load by relieving him of some zip-ties and wish him luck.

Returning inside, I discover I've caught up with a friend of my training buddy. We've traded a few texts through Facebook. He's been here since the control opened and has spent the interim in undisturbed slumber. That beats the hell out my 90 minute snatch and I am very envious of his apparent freshness.

As the 24 hour mark rolls around, I can see that the battle against the clock is going to be won or lost in controls. I'd love to stay and talk with the stream of cyclists arriving, but am already aware that at least three shifts have run through and left whilst I've been milling about. I also recognise that my original plan to ride in the day and sleep at night is wildly out of shape. I figure I'm good for two more controls before I drop and hope that this will sync me up loosely to what was once a circadian rhythm. Been out of the saddle for an hour now, time to get going.

Monday 1447 hours
Time elapsed: 24 hours. Miles travelled: 256.
Day plans abandoned: 1.

Serious hills to the north, and I'm grateful we skirt west around the worst of them. Gradual climbs from Sowerby, pulling first west then directly north. South Otterington, Newby Wiske, Warlaby, Yafforth, Sweden Sykes. Hills to west and east, but north clear for the time being. Through Langton, Kiplin, Bolton on Swale, Scorton, slowly gaining height.

The road starts to climb considerably as we enter the final few miles, and I'm tickled to see that the North Yorkshire villages of Moulton and Brompton are less than 2 miles apart. Twenty odd instructions have taken me to Middleton Tyas, and I swing into the school that is hosting our control.

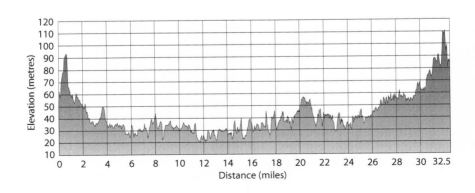

Monday 1710hrs
Miles travelled: 290. At Middleton Tyas Control.

Odd how the controls retain their character. The purposed architecture bleeds into the mood of the riders and volunteers. Controls in community centres are noticeably chatty environments. Those in village halls are slightly more formal, with structured morals underpinned by dusty austere hierarchies. Middleton Tyas is in a school. We are efficiently ticketed, served a plate of food and set out in rows. At this stage, being ushered around like a five-year-old is very comforting and accurately matches my inability to process information independently. Within 30 minutes I've been fed, watered, recharged and am headed back to the bike.

10% of my brain tells me I really need to sleep before trying to tackle the Pennines. 90 minutes' kip in 35 hours is neither conducive to stamina or concentration. Another 10% says I need to go now or risk steering for the Yad Moss summit in the dark. If the clock wasn't ticking, I'd get my head down now and set off just before first light. Stopping, however, is not a luxury I have. I wait a few minutes to see if the remaining 80% of my mind has an opinion either way, but it's locked up mumbling something about my knees. I decide to ignore it until it can at least be more eloquent.

Monday 1743hrs
Pennines, Cattle Grids and Sheep (oh my).

Looks like it'll be a sunny evening. I lower myself delicately back onto the 'bent and set the GPS for the route ahead. From the overview screen I see that where I sit is only 20 miles from the East Coast and the North Sea. 27 instructions later I'm going to be less than 15 from the Irish Sea, due north of Carlisle and on the other side of the country. Between there and here are The Pennines, Yad Moss, Cumbria and the highest market town in England. All of these fall in the next leg.

Of course, later on I'll be steering for Edinburgh, back on the East coast, the wrong side of the Southern Uplands, and in an entirely other country altogether, but it doesn't pay to dwell on these things. Looks like it's going to get bumpy from here on in.

This, then, is the stage I've been fearing the most. A long drag into the hilliest terrain I'm likely to ever encounter on a 'bent. Thus far I've been bumbling around between 20 and 100m above sea level. This one will take me to 600m above, before trying to descend on cobbles. Hills always thresh the recumbents out from the uprights, and I've been riding on my own through the worst of the terrain to date. I don't fancy this one alone.

Come on. It's only going to get darker, so let's be off. Duck under the A1. Climb to 150m through Melsonby. Field-bordered undulations through Forcett and Caldwell play with the top 50, robbing it from me, then throwing it back into my path repeatedly.

At Whorton the road suddenly pitches down into a deep ravine. The tarmac manages to hold on as the GPS alerts me of a 'Care: Wooden Bridge'. As I roll onto it, I can imagine this would get pretty slippery in the wet.

Not for me though. The low sun treats us[12] to a river reflecting pure gold. The shadows are long and the green of the countryside responds in beautiful swansong. It's a wonderful sight and utterly distracts me from the imminent climb. Very imminent, as it turns out. The bridge meets the other side of the ravine some way short of the top and a horrendous switchback makes sufficient demands on legs that I have to take more than one run at it. Until I finally steam into the village my world is inverse cambered sharp turns ON steep climbs.

With Whorton safely behind me, I'm riding into the sun through Westwick and Barnard Castle. Climbing out to Lartington, through Cotherstone. I'm reviewing a wide choice of peaks up front, trying to work out which is Yad Moss. The climb is steady and scenic. I make a note to come back here with Evey one day, though preferably in a car. Sharp rise before Romaldkirk, and I'm fenced in by summits. Mickleton, and Middleton in Teesdale line me up for a big climb, but the route swings left before I can really get stuck into it. We hang onto the side of the hill, gradually hauling ourselves up to New Biggin (250m) and Forest in Teesdale (376m). Just past Langdon Beck the gradient really commits and lifts me to 450m.

I'm perched on the left hand edge of a huge rise and am trying to trace the tail lights of support vehicles as they make their way past me and onwards. Does the road go right up this thing? Is there a bigger hill ahead? Am I even on Yad Moss yet?

---

12   *For any moderately hilly section, 'us' is me and the bike. 'We' is me and my knees.*

Broad warnings of cattle grids and animals in the road keep me on my toes and I vow that I've got to reach the safety of the control whilst there's still some ambient light. Rolling across a grid at 12mph mightn't be fatal but this is really not the place for a puncture.

High force is simply stunning and I am moved by its raw beauty. I'm tracing back up the river Tees, its speed raising as mine slows. I seem to be climbing as quickly as the sun is setting and spend an hour in perpetual twilight. There are plenty of false summits as the road winds left and right, but the distance to next waypoint: "YM Peak" shows the climb will end imminently. The wind picks up as I winch myself to 597m. The horizon opens out and I am evidently on top of the world.

The road sheds light, warmth and altitude rapidly, and I am utterly depleted. I night ride enough to know when I'm done, and I'm feeling it now. The road isn't lit, there are animals on it, frozen fingers clutch at brakes and I edge down erratically between 26 and 10mph. I daren't let the bike roll free and am concentrating on keeping her in the middle of the road. Reactions are well down and there are soft verges with long drops.

As the road snakes back down, tiny spots of white appear in my mirror. Angels, perhaps? They get closer and I'm treated to a fly-by. How sophisticated: Angels on bicycles. Three or four of them, I think. Must try harder to end my time in heaven.

I ease off a little, waiting for the treachery of cobbles, and see the angels suddenly swing skywards up ahead. Looks like there's one more climb before I join them. My guess is they roll it on momentum alone, but I'm doing 7mph and have to crank up on my knees.

Just before 10pm I'm waved left off the road and arrive at Alston control. The angels' bikes are parked up around the side.

Monday 2202hrs
Miles Travelled: 334.
Alstons arrived: 1. Cobbles encountered: 0.

The angels have been here for 10 minutes or so. We trade stories. They'd had to sit on their brakes until I was going straight enough to pass and hadn't pedalled at all for the last six miles. They also seem to be able to coordinate legs and arms and are in considerably better shape than me. Turns out they even noticed that whilst checkpoint and cobbles are both in Alston, the control comes first. Important distinction and probably added 20+ mins to my time on the way in.

No bother. Grab some food. Wash it down with sugary tea. Lovely. By the time I'm done, its gone 11. The tiny dining room is now absolutely full of cyclists and I'm eager to slip away before the competition for sleeping space gets critical.

Whispers move through the group. I hear fables of an upstairs lounge, a concealed staircase above the kitchen, a hallowed Shangri-la of scatter cushions, carpet and sofas. I edge away from the eaters, making my way towards the exit as discreetly as possible.

Dropping out of sight, I clamber up. When I finally emerge into the vista at the top, I feel like a disillusioned backpacker who has roamed through the jungle for three days to get off the beaten track, only to emerge into a clearing featuring a McDonalds and a Butlins.

The room looks like a scene from The Somme. Body parts splay unnaturally over every horizontal surface, legs rest up against walls, their owners buried under the combined detritus of tired randonneurs. The occasional strobe flashes the room as another cyclist piles in behind me, head torch still on, seeking out an inch of carpet. Childhood skills learnt playing 'Operation' and 'Kerplunk' are called into action trying to get across the biomass.

Midnight passes but sleep eludes me. The kitchen continues in full flow downstairs. Provision of food seems to be mediated through loud percussion. Pans slam together to an accompaniment of shouting. In four hours I will have breakfast at their grace, but even knowing it is a terrible thought, I dearly wish they would just shut up.

This is the hardest bit, with no doubt. I revise the alarm to give me 180 minutes sleep, put my ear on the Blackberry and try to drown out the snores. I am so tired I can actually hear the whine of my brain drying out.

After an age, I retreat into the climbs of this morning. The road ascends in sunshine, under trees. White lines reach out to me, passing under my wheels with a light hum. Eventually the space between the lines grows. The tree cover robs more of the sunlight. The hum becomes constant. Wind noise dies away. I coast along a grey road of sleep.

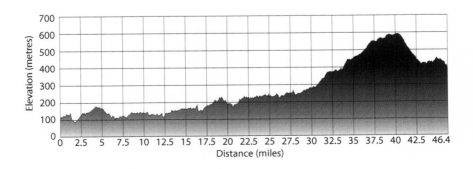

LEL Day 3:
Tuesday

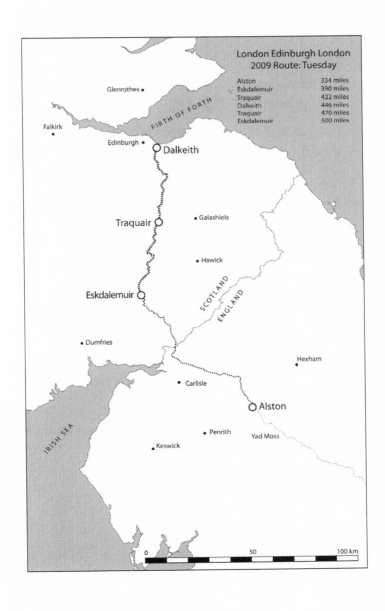

London Edinburgh London
2009 Route: Tuesday

Alston	334 miles
Eskdalemuir	390 miles
Traquair	422 miles
Dalkeith	446 miles
Traquair	470 miles
Eskdalemuir	500 miles

Tuesday 0418hrs
Ski Hire?

I wake just before the alarm sings out, silence it, and spot a soon-to-be-vacated bit of sofa. I wait. Quietly. Wake no-one. Drop in behind the departing cyclist immediately on exit and grab an additional and much-needed hour's kip. Clock rolls around to 05:15, get up. Sys check says things are OK. Probably got around three hours' sleep. Self-test brain over breakfast with attempts to do the maths on arrivals versus closing times for controls on my brevet card.

- 1 hour 15minutes down at start
- Either out of time, or irretrievably lost, at Gamlingay
- 3 hours 51 minutes up by Thurlby
- 6 hours 9 minutes up by Washingborough
- 6 hours 30 minutes up by Wragby (short leg)
- 9 hours 37 minutes up at Thorne
- 10 hours 39 minutes in Coxwold
- 11 hours 25 minutes at Middleton Tyas
- 12 hours 53 minutes up on arrival to Alston.

That's good. I made time, even on that last leg. If I can keep that pace going, I need only keep about four hours in the bag to deal with punctures, zip-ties and mechanicals. Assuming nothing too daft, I can take a fairly relaxed breakfast, or, better still, grab a sleep somewhere on the way out from Scotland. My legs are probably even fresh.

By the time I've processed food and figures, its coming up 0630. Just under four and a half hours in the bag. Still safe.

I exit by the side door, noting the sign for ski-hire. Ski-hire? Surely a clear indicator that this is not an intelligent place to arrive by bike...

Tuesday 0635hrs
Leaving Alston: Back on the road.

Climbing back up to the main road, it is immediately obvious that the prior few hours have not given my knees time to repair. Being distracted by hallucinations and exhaustion, I'd somehow forgotten that they were really hurting. In the cold light of morning, every crank slides another freezing dagger under the patella. I consider getting off and walking the remaining 200yds to the ongoing route. This is not good. At all.

I make a left at the top of the path and begin to roll down towards the town. I'm hoping another few minutes' rest stolen from the incline will see some improvement. I let my feet hang in the pedals, but when I resume it feels even worse. I decide that the only way to keep sane is to maintain a low and easy cadence whilst coasting.

I opt to walk down the cobbles, which keeps me from the attentions of the puncture fairy. Many have blogged on this part of the route. Estimates vary from 14 to 20% incline. Let's just say "it's steep". If pushed, I'll add "and bumpy". On the outbound route it's not a problem anyway. Particularly if walking. Knees don't hurt so bad when I'm not pushing pedals.

Roll over the bridge and begin to climb towards 'Raise'. This is less than a mile into my day. Pedalling is on the edge of prohibitively painful. I determine that with my current chain configuration, the cranks are mechanically inefficient. It would be far simpler to just grind cartilage from my knees directly into the bottom bracket as a paste. I push as far as I can, then come to a halt. I sit for a few minutes.

The beauty of LEL is that you get the chance to really test yourself. You take yourself to a point where your body screams "STOP!" Your brain provides all kinds of reasons as to why you shouldn't go on. I'm sat at the edge of a cold grey road, listening to myself reason that continuing in this state might do enough damage to take me off the bike permanently. That there's more at risk than some arbitrary distance and time. That this pain might be something that never goes away. I've been in this position before. It is not a happy place. For all her apparent cruelty, LEL will always do her best to protect you by ensuring these moments happen 50 odd miles from the nearest station. Whilst eminently desirable, dropping out now is only a hypothetical discussion. If I can't go on, I'm stuck at the side of this road forever. If I can go on, I damn well will.

Sitting with one foot on the pedal, I can sense that it hurts 'less' if I extend my leg further, rocking back on my heel. Same for the other foot too.

Hmmmm... Given it'll make no odds if I'm pushing the bike anyway, I resolve to extend the boom a little. I grab the Allen keys from the seat bag and relax things by two full turns. The previously millimetre perfect adjustments are discarded as I simply push the boom out with my foot clipped in until it feels "about right". Maybe an inch and a half. Give it a wiggle until the derailleur mast is aimed loosely skywards, then set about re-clamping it.

No manufacturer's specific torque wrench settings for me. Two full turns back and I call it secure. Stand bike upright, realise 'skywards' is relative to the lean of the frame, redo it to the 12 o'clock position, clip in and wobble away. Hurts less. Seems good. Stop. Remember to close the seat bag. Go again. All good. Yes.

The road from here ambles up and down between 250 and 300m, refusing to settle on the valley floor through Slaggyford and Knarsdale. Knees are hurting less now but I know the clock is still closing on me. I envy the river, which now sits to my right, idly checking off a schedule that features a single entry, some 5000 years from now; "Ox-bow lake?"

We part company at Lambley. She wanders on for a bit, before ambling east to Newcastle, whilst I swing due west to meet her baby sister in Midgeholme. The valley opens out at Hallbankgate and the wind lets up long enough for me to spot a nice gradient. Legs are getting better now and I speed through Milton and on to my first route instruction in 30km. By the time my GPS chimes in, I've completely forgotten that I'm even on an audax.

Brampton sees a brief climb to Newtown (knees OK) and I'm in flat lands again. Without the GPS altitude read out, I'd swear I'm on top of some huge plateau. The winds are constant, the air seems thin, the pale sun does nothing to stave off the cold. Considering I'm sat at only 15m above, I seem to have got very short shrift from the descent.

I am literally making mountains out of molehills and battle up and down a glass flat surface to Longtown. The reduced pace and spartan route instructions (three for 60km?) mean I've been taking in more of my immediate environs. Road signs over the last few miles have been just getting funnier – Carlisle? Gretna? – but six miles along the A7 I spot a real winner: "Welcome to Scotland".

I can't resist pulling over and trying to revive my phone. A text gets through to those at home:

"41hrs, 28 mins. That's what it takes to ride from London to Scotland."

This gives me a good psychological boost. I could stop here and get a great sleep and still roll into Scotland within 48 hours from home. On a bicycle. Whatever happens from here on in, that's a hell of an achievement and I can go back with my head held high.

With ego secured, I set about closing on the hills up ahead. As the valley sides steepen around me, I find myself tracing the Esk northwards, crossing Skippers Bridge just before 10am. I'm still elated, but sense that the river beneath me is increasingly grey and angry. Surrounded by a blackened tree line, lumps of rock are churned up and spat out by the livid currents. The weather has beaten the colour out of everything. Houses, foliage, earth, even stone are no match for these hostile hinterlands.

Tracing The Esk

With trepidation I pedal onwards, through Langholm, then north-west with the river to Bentpath. Although I'm climbing as I go, this is nothing compared to the intimidation of the landscape around me. Bullied some 18,000 years back by the retreating ice age, one gets the feeling Scotland has never quite gotten over it and is out for revenge on anyone not quite smart enough to bring shelter and an engine. If this turns, it is going to get majorly ugly, very quickly.

Penultimate instruction now (Potholes, Cattle Grids, Animals) translates to a long drag up along a timber route. The evident scarring to the landscape is a wake-up to me. Back in the South, we buy our wood in flat-pack Scandinavian kits, planed and packaged to carefully conceal anything as base as a tree in its origins. The damage doesn't stop at the edge of the road either. Its integrated into the surface. Discarded chips, branches, bits of bark, loose gravel and crumbling corners are all present. Given we're less than 65 miles East of John Macadam's birth-place, I'm suspecting he never took a wander this way. Huge and sudden climb when I'm about three miles out, then drop back down to 200m and roll into Eskdalemuir. Cross the river once again and there's the control on the left.

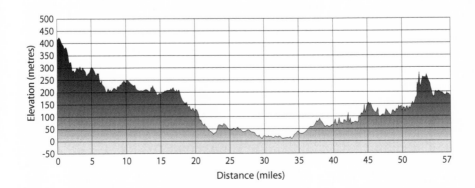

Tuesday 1106hrs
Arrive Eskdalemuir: 390+ miles.
44 hours. 21 minutes.
What no Buddhists?

I've been looking forward to this control, as the photos from the 2005 LEL suggest it is either inside or adjacent to a Buddhist temple. I am confronted by what appears to be an utterly typical village hall.

I mask my disappointment and allow myself an hour to fill water bottle and stomach. Tired fingers fumble at laces. Want to be out just after midday if I'm going to make the 100+ mile run to Traquair, Dalkeith and back. I'm still pulling around 17mph on the flats but these are now few and far between. Life is a little confusing.

I check the zip-ties, freshening one that is wearing through, replacing another that dropped off somewhere on the last descent. I am pleased to see one of Rich Forrest's ties has made it with me all the way from Coxwold. Still going strong, so I leave it in place as a good luck charm.

Despite heroics of the few, the bag is once again running low. I am extremely surprised when, just before leaving, I am confronted by YACFer Mal Volio who gives me another 100. These forumites get everywhere!

Trusting that these will now see me good for the remaining 48 hours and 500 odd miles, I set off for Traquair.

Tuesday 1209hrs
Depart Eskdalemuir for Traquair.

Quick review of where things are on the GPS before I set off. This should be a quick one. At 30 miles, its half the length of the previous stage, and looks to be similar terrain. I'm figuring I'll be in Traquair just after two.

(Worth noting here that my GPS is the base model 'Legend' and does not have the altitude graph of the 'Vista'.)

A closer zoom reveals the route ahead is peppered with regular 90 degree zig zags, three miles on a side. This is exactly the strategy I would take if I were sailing into the wind or trying to avoid U-boats. On land, however, it means hills. Lots of hills.

Best get off if I'm going to keep schedule. Less than a minute along the road I'm spotting ribbons tied to occasional trees. These give way to the formalised spacing of Tibetan prayer flags – carrying blessings of compassion, wisdom, strength and peace with the wind. Shortly afterwards these are overtaken by the Liberation Gate of the Kagyu Samye Ling Tibetan Centre. Under a grey sky, the view is positively other-worldly. A statue of Nagarjuna floats in a lake, under a giant snake. Guru Rinpoche is seated upon a lotus flower. The Victory Stupa reaches out to the wayfaring cyclists, transforming any negative energies and restoring balance to all who pass. A very useful trait on a recumbent. My mantra of gratitude, "Left Pedal. Right Pedal."

Climb up to Davington, cross the White Esk, bridge myriad sike and burn to emerge on the north bank of Loch Tima. Continue north-east along Tima water, the ridges towering 100m above me to left and right. North again, across the ford at Ramseycleugh to Ettrick Water, then follow the valley floor to a sharp west turn with Tulshielaw Burn. Do not stray from the river.

As I winch my way up, the broken lands of Black Knowe Head and The Wiss swell two hundred metres above me in a 45 degree slope. It feels like being buried alive. Before coming to Scotland, I have never felt claustrophobic outdoors.

The horizon continues to push in on me and I am relieved when I finally exit the pass at Yarrow Water. Crossing the A708, the pattern repeats. The routesheet is as barren as the landscape.

As the hills build up again, I am left with absolute wonder that Traquair is settled at all. The confidence or conditions required to push people north through this are incomprehensible to me. Although the instructions are simple (follow the B709 from the last control to next), without the GPS I would certainly be lost. It is she that puts names to places, captions to peaks, labels on rivers. In cataloguing them, ownership is implied. Mankind has stamped his authority on the landscape, and I no longer feel that it will take me.

Spotting a radio mast at Mountbenger, civilisation sprints 500 years forwards; I discover I have phone reception for the first time since crossing the border. I struggle with the battery and manage to get an SMS through to David at Laid Back Bikes of Edinburgh. He replies, offering to meet me at the Dalkeith control with a replacement idler borrowed from one of his stock bikes. I begin to feel human, just being momentarily in contact with someone.

The sun comes out as I climb the final hill. Suspicious of the clock, I switch zip-ties and push hard to reach the descent. As the road first levels, then tilts down, I close the remaining miles to the control at an average 27mph.

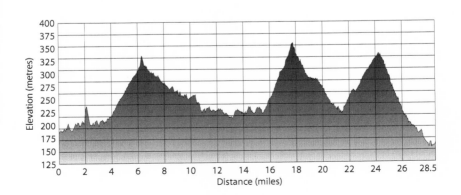

Tuesday 1418hrs
422 Miles, Arrive Traquair.

A Scotsman in a kilt stands in the middle of the road waving me in. I park up, grab water bottle and brevet card, and head indoors. There are a handful of riders sprinkled around the tables. This close to the halfway point, people are not hanging around. There are two microwaves on the stage, a LEL cake and numerous bowls of porridge. A young boy picks up a bowl and hands it to me. "Salt or Whisky?"

I deny either, giving it a liberal dose of sugar intended for tea. Alcohol does not seem a good idea right now. I am surprised how hungrily I wolf down the porridge, given I stuffed myself silly only a couple of hours earlier. This terrain burns a lot of calories. With a nod to the clock, I'm standing outside in bright sunlight 15 minutes later, clambering aboard the bike once more and targeting Dalkeith.

Tuesday 1436hrs
Across the Moorfoot Hills

I claim a goodbye wave from the be-kilted and am dazzled by the transformation to mood that a little sunshine and food will do. Looking around I find I am in a hidden valley, 160m above sea level, surrounded by stunning peaks.

There are barely 25 miles between me and Dalkeith, and whilst the hills close in once again on the tiny road as it winds northwards, I am amazed to find myself crossing a near perfectly level Innerleithen Golf Course. The closely flanking slopes surely prevent a ball straying too far from the fairway, but there is no doubt that the rising breeze is making it hard going for the handful of players.

I remember checking this leg before I left and know there are two big climbs up ahead, one around 370m, the other above 400m. Two miles out the first climb begins. The valley narrows, the little road is bounced around wildly between domineering bens, the valley floor is pinched down to a river's width, then slowly raised skywards.

Eight miles in, I hit the top of the first peak. The wind continues to rise and I am down to ~7mph going full tilt. Although the next two and a half miles are a pretty steep descent, the wind forces me to push hard on the pedals just to keep moving. The thought of coming back on this road a few hours hence, with the wind behind me, keeps my spirits up. I am also gaining a much needed mental lift from the increasing numbers of returning riders greeting me on the road. I have spent much of the last 420 miles on my own and it is wonderful to be in the company of other cyclists, even if we're passing each other at closing speeds of 35mph. I spot GerryC in a group of four or so, and not far behind them my LongHairedScouser.

One more climb in a strong side wind and I am finally rewarded with a view that takes in Lammer Law, West Lomond, Arthur's Seat, Leith, Dunfermline and the Firth of Forth. Somewhere beneath me is Dalkeith, and (even better) there are ten miles of freshly surfaced tarmac to reel it in.

The B7007 to Dalkeith

As the descent opens up my mood begins to change. For the first time in the last two days I start fearing the return leg. I've been dropping like a Stuka for five miles now, hovering around the 37mph mark, and watching southbound randonneurs blip past me on the climb. No more waving. This is white knuckle all the way.

It is stunningly beautiful but I cannot even begin to consider how I'm going to get back up. "All downhills must be earned" rings in my ears and I know I definitely prefer to pay in advance.

As countryside slowly concedes its grip, I hope to hell that Dalkeith will come soon. I join the A7 and am treated to yet another sickening plunge, way down, down past the mining museum my wife has a bookmark from, down between lorries and buses, down through road markings, bus stops, streetlamps, a series of roundabouts. My ears pop against the city's roar, I am building speed all the way.

The GPS beeps with 500ft to go and I brake heavy to slide into the control at 11 minutes past 4.

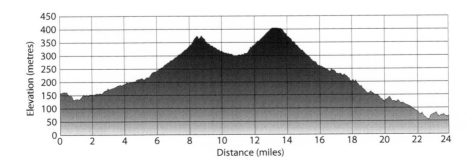

Tuesday 1611hrs
49 Hours, 26 Minutes, 446 miles.
Dalkeith Control.

Definite air of relief indoors as we reach the halfway point. The motorcycle support riders are here too, and the camaraderie is evident. It's sunny outside and we know there will be no surprise hills on the route back south. The organisers have allowed entrants to arrange a small bag drop at Dalkeith. Mine has a change of clothes, some energy bars, a couple of inner tubes and a few gels. It is testament to the quality of provisions at each control that I do not need to replenish anything I have brought with me. I even consider shedding the six cereal bars I've carried the last ~450 miles, but decide these don't weigh much and might just save me later on.

I grab some food and allow myself to process the previous 50 hours since leaving Lea Valley. I'm ahead of schedule and have around 2 days, 18 hours to get back to London. Curiosities of the routing around Gainsborough mean my return leg will be almost 20 miles shorter and I consider adding to the 40 minutes I've already spent here with a few hours kip and a wash.

Once again, I'm caught by the lump in my schedule that is nightfall. It'll take at least three hours to get through Traquair, and maybe another two to get to Eskdalemuir. Whilst the sun and I are high in the sky now, it is almost 5pm. After sundown the pass is going to be pretty cold. As an option, Alston is maybe reachable by 2am, but I daren't tackle Yad Moss in the dark again. Best bet will be to head out of here in the next few minutes, get myself to the next control and make a call on it. If it's dry, I can push on and sleep at Alston until sun up. If not, I'll grab whatever I can at Eskdalemuir and head off a couple of hours before dawn. This all sounds suitably achievable, and I trek back out to the 'bent once more.

Tuesday 1703hrs
Exit Dalkeith. I'm coming home.

As I clamber back up the A7, I am treated to the confidence-inducing sight of northbound riders coming my way. I almost definitely started after each one that I see and remember passing many of them in prior stages. The mood is friendly and waves float towards me from each group. Audaxing is not a competitive event.

I know from the ride in that the next ten miles will see me climb to 400m and I pitch myself into the hill with renewed legs. Over the next five miles, my 17mph at the bottom gradually drops to a little over 6. It's all distance clocked off though, and I am also finding this is the most sociable part of the ride so far. Whilst a loaded recumbent isn't ideal for hill-climbing, the advantages of lower wind resistance mean I'm climbing at about the same speed as the uprights.

As the headwind continues to rip into us, I spend a happy couple of miles trading places in a two man chain-gang. No words are spoken. All energies are directed towards the pedals. Although the going is easier I know this is slower than I would travel under my own power, so with some regret I pull away from my only riding partner of the event so far and force myself up the remaining slope alone.

Just before a quarter past six I reach the second peak. Cresting as the road kinks left then right, I am greeted by the wind rushing up the southern side of the summit. The force of it near stops me in my tracks and I wobble to a halt, dropping another couple of gears.

The view to the south across the Moorfoot Hills is equally impressive, not least because most of it is downhill. This time I descend into an emerging valley, losing altitude to the continued peaks that flank me. The wind is alternately behind me, to the side, slamming into my front, pushing me off the road. I greet oncoming randonneurs with shouts of "one more hill!" but their replies are stolen by the gale.

Short climb at Dewar, then descend to join Leithen Water at Colquhar. I know I'm almost there when I see the golf course and take the chance, once again, to marvel at the tenacity of players now hacking their way up the back nine, 40 yards at a time.

More oncoming cyclists as I cross the river on the approach to Innerleithen, and again on the way out. The wind whips the sunshine away to drizzle and a few minutes later I am huddled at the edge of the road, clambering into the Traquair Control for shelter.

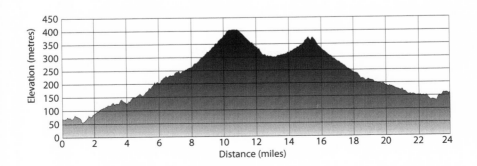

Tuesday 1914hrs
Traquair Southbound.
64 hours remaining. 402 miles to go...

I know the routine by now and manage to grab my own porridge. The bulk of riders here are headed south, but all are beginning to look a little ragged. One lady introduces herself to me by way of "Do you have any pro-plus?"

As I'm packing a box of 48 in the seat bag and have only used four, I tell her I likely have a few outside she can take. I am a little taken aback when she takes this response to mean "Please dive into my pack and rummage through until you find what you need," but understand that necessity outranks protocol. I take a few minutes to sort the bag back into some semblance of order, which affords me discovery of an additional five zip-ties that had filtered their way out of sight. This reminds me... I didn't manage to arrange to meet David with that idler. Damn.

Oh well, the ties have held thus far, and I know how to fix them if something happens. I'm happy to rely on the current solution a while longer. Right. Where'd that lady go?

I trail my caffeine supply back to a table indoors, and get a proper introduction to Deniece and her companions: Tomsk of YACF and a Lithuanian called Rimas. I join the conversation and discover that Deniece was an early starter and is thus facing a curfew some six hours earlier than mine at Lea Valley. She's in a bad way and with only two hours' grace cannot afford to rest here. Tom seems committed to getting her through the next few stages and I hear that they plan to hit Alston before sleep.

Outside the wind has continued to build and those with time in hand are opting to wait in and see if it blows out. I'm not so sure it's going to do much else but rain for the night and figure if I'm going to get wet anyway I might as well do it in the light. That said, the day is fading fast and I take a 'safety in numbers' approach of joining the exiting pace-line whilst I can.

Tuesday 1936hrs
Depart Traquair. Into the storm

As we set off, I first try to stay with, then within 200 yards, of the group. I'm happy to take my time at the front, but low slung on the 'bent I'm not offering much shelter to the person behind me. Tom and I are tackling things at about the same speed and its only when he pulls in front that I realise... he's riding FIXED![13]

South through Kirkhouse, trees to my left, fields to the right. Sunlight dies in shades of grey and the pack huddle in for the climb. An inky blackness steals the stars.

...Meanwhile, to the south-east, the Met Office issues Cumbria with a severe weather warning. Residents are advised not to make any unnecessary journeys...

We drop into Mountbenger, then climb due east towards Crosslee. Our phones are dead. It's slow going. The GPS is unlit, only waking itself up for the occasional turn. The rising rain is beating into our faces, but we figure we can push through. Less than 30 miles to go. The deluge builds. A Cimmerian curtain cloaks us. As I stop beside Tom and wait for the others, we realise water is beginning to fill the valley.

...To the north-west a tornado hits Stornaway. Windows are smashed, cars are flipped, the grid fails...

---

13   A bicycle equipped with a single gear and no freewheel, meaning the pedals are always in motion when the bicycle is moving. Normally selected for its mechanical purity, enhanced communion of rider and machine, or paired with skinny jeans, an iPod and an ironic T-shirt to gain inclusion with the urban 'messenger' scene.

Between the two, our little troupe. Time stops. Everything becomes meaningless. I read afterwards that the headwind was pushing us back at +60kph, gusting at twice that. For the moment, we are blind, pedalling against a solid wall of rain. Prayers stolen from Kagyu Samye Ling crash through the valley, tearing at our faces before being lost to the maelstrom around us. For two hours I focus only on keeping with the rider in front, little red lights dancing like bubbles of oxygen, just out of reach. White dragons unfurl behind our wheels, formations of white chevrons tailing us. Nobody dares slow down. Nobody dares stop. 10 feet apart, I see no one for 20 miles.

At twenty to eleven we catch the flicker of electric light to our left. The control is upon us. We pull up, exhausted, hypothermic, drenched through. Hands fumble, limbs fail. We stand in the rain because we can't remember to get inside. In a moment of horror, we find we are only two. Somewhere behind, Rimas and Deniece continue to fight their way through the dark towards us.

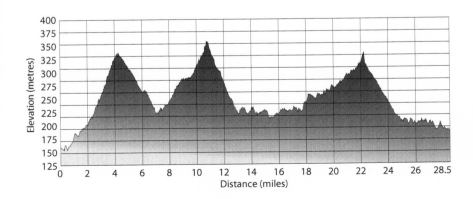

Tuesday 2242hrs
500 miles. Sanctuary.

We check in with the desk, brevet cards disintegrating even within their plastic bags. The field is wrecked. 20 riders have stopped. 33 are missing. We are locked down, schedules marred by the storm. Ahead of us, riders have been blown off the road at Alston. Behind us, nobody is leaving Traquair. Blankets are borrowed and wrapped around the few straggling arrivers. Cyclists sleep under tables, on chairs, perched on window ledges, as they queue. A single heater in the middle of the room struggles under a complex shanty of wet clothes. My hands don't work. I will not stop shivering. The floor is lost under puddles wrung from drenched lycra. Riders and joists buckle under the onslaught. We are spent.

Senses are mugged by barbed aroma combining damp clothes, sweaty bodies and muscle rub. It has the smell of ginger beer and menthol, tastes like gravel, sounds like a shrill whistle. Through the onslaught, Rimas makes his way to our table. Exhaustion deprives him of language. Deniece arrives maybe five minutes behind. She is visibly shaken. Pale as a two year old, now sobbing with relief. There are not enough blankets. We put her near the fire, but nobody is warming up.

Tom has slumped onto the table. It is near midnight. One of the volunteers approaches me.

"I have a room. A spare bed. Are you together?" She motions towards Deniece.

"No".

"I have another bed. It's only a single. You could sleep there."

[I've lost the power of speech]

"I'm sorry. It's not as comfortable."

[Comfort is relative]

"What about him? The older gentleman?" now gesturing towards another shivering rider.

Over the next few minutes, she coaxes a handful of us towards the door. Although the promise of a warm bed beckons, movement still takes too much energy to do with any waste.

"How far is your house?" asks Deniece.

"Three doors down. It's very close. I have radiators. I can dry your clothes."

The storm continues outside. Cold fingers pull at wet laces. We struggle to force swollen feet back into rain saturated shoes.

"I can't." says Deniece.

"Here, wear mine"

And with that our unknown rescuer leads us from the village hall, barefoot through the storm to her house, rigs hot drinks for Deniece, Roy and myself, apologises again for the lack of space, sets the heating to max and prepares sleeping arrangements for all three of us.

Having surrended her own room to Deniece, Roy and I are offered the spare. There is a single bed, and whilst I'm happy to sleep on carpet (dry, warm and soft, it looks perfect) she insists I allow her to unfold a padded massage table. This done, she briefly exits the room to collect a set of sheets, and I clamber up onto it, going to sleep immediately.

Our host quietly moves our clothes to the radiator, checks in with Deniece as to what time we need waking, throws a sheet over me and pads back to the heaving control, where she spends the rest of the night making drinks, providing food and collecting riders.

Her voice wakes me some hours later. I am warm and comfortable, surrounded by Tibetan curiosities, floating high above the floor. My clothes are dry, my shoes stuffed with newspaper. I can hear the rain continue outside. Within the shelter of warm covers, its rhythm is reassuring.

I slowly lower myself from the table and gain momentary confusion as I attempt to locate my socks. I recall trying to dry them at the control, but haven't seen them since. If they're not retrievable from the furnace, I'll buy some on the road. Manners restored by a few hours' rest, I introduce myself to our landlady and thank her for her kindness. As I tiptoe out, careful not to wake the riders now spilling from every corner of her house, she spots my bare ankles.

Four minutes later at the control she re-appears with a pair of men's socks. In my size. Before 4am. In a village with maybe 20 houses. Unworn and still wrapped. The good people of Eskdalemuir are legend.

Determined to preserve my newly dry state, I claim a couple of bin bags, pink and lightly scented, and put one on either foot before putting my shoes back on. Another gets holes for arms and head, and is called into service as a featherlite disposable gilet. Worn between base layer and windproof jacket, I am now almost waterproof up top. I am learning quickly.

I rejoin Rimas and Tom. The ceiling has leaked during the night. Deniece and I have fared considerably better than the riders remaining at the control. We regroup, grab a quick breakfast and resolve to set off as soon as the rain outside quietens a little. At 0420 our opportunity arises.

Photo: Tom Deakins

LEL Day 4: Wednesday

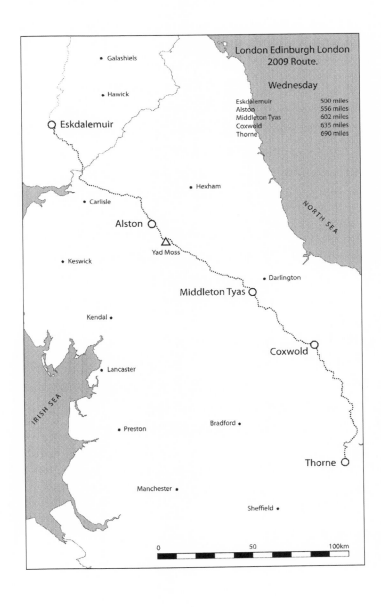

London Edinburgh London 2009 Route.

Wednesday

Eskdalemuir	500 miles
Alston	556 miles
Middleton Tyas	602 miles
Coxwold	635 miles
Thorne	690 miles

Wednesday 0424hrs
55 hours remaining. 372 miles to cover.

I return to the 'bent. Even in the darkness I can detect that things the previous night were not merely wet. The entire bottom half of my bike is coated in what looks like river silt. I crack the worst of the silver grey carapace from the chain, get the links moving reasonably freely and hop aboard for another 60 miles to Alston. Should be there around 1030hrs.

We cross the White Esk exiting the control, tracing its eastern bank back into the glens. The rain continues but has lost most of its anger by now. Having survived last night, the ongoing downpour doesn't seem to register. It might be because I'm wrapped in plastic, or could be because the general lack of sleep from the previous few days now insulates me against most sensation.

The occasional crunch of gravel under tyre punctuates the otherwise monotonous rattling of my chain. The sound is so familiar that I am no more aware of it than I am the sound of blood rushing around my ears. Outside our tiny group, the world is a still frame.

The sun is due up around 4:35, but we don't see it until the road lifts us another 100m beyond Allangill Burn, offering a view south-east that takes in the summits of Carlesgill and Crumpton Hill. Seven miles on, our onward route will pass between these peaks, but for now we drop back down to rejoin the Esk through Bentpath.

Stray fingers of sunlight edge through the valleys ahead, pulling back on the peaks, slowly stretching open the horizon. Laid flat on the 'bent, a foot from the floor, the experience conjures emotions of deliverance. The sky lightens, my mood is raised.

We continue south-east, slowly filtering through glen and dale to arrive in Langholm at 0544. Even at this time, The Muckle Toonfolk are beginning their day's activities. I had forgotten people did things other than cycle, and am so surprised that I stop and spend six minutes just watching them.

A quick exploration of Langholm's former library gardens reveals little scope for a nature break, but does uncover a discarded arch, completed by a stonemason's apprentice in the 1760s. Local lad, name of Thomas Telford, apparently. The absolute lack of signage suggests the town enjoys either a dearth of visitors or an abundance of such history.

Exiting on the A7 between Warb Law and Monument Hill, I am done with what Scotland has to throw at me. My mood is celebratory, and the loss of concentration immediately triggers a minor routing mishap, up the eastern bank of Ryehills, on a busy dual carriageway. Inadvisable excursions aside, I get one more short climb into Canonbie, and then it's a gentle roll all the way down the hill, to a little brown sign, tucked into the hedge, "Welcome to ENGLAND".

0639hrs. I'm south of the border, west of the sun. The towering giants that have crowded on every side these last few hundred miles finally retreat. Their rain-cloaked peaks fall out of sight behind me as the landscape slowly unfurls, restoring the horizon to its rightful place, at eye level, and some distance hence. I am glad to make it out. 30 miles behind me, riders making their way from Traquair to Eskdalemuir are fighting through the residue of last night's assault. Photos later shared reveal the B709 is lost under standing water, cyclists blindly feeling their way along the camber at Ettrick, whilst alluvial detritus washes over hub and sprocket.

Riders at Ettrick. Wednesday morning.
Photo: Clive Handy

Mere drizzle for me though. I reel in Longtown, arriving via the celebrated 18th Century bridge, to cross the Esk one final time. From here, she will run west, joining Lyne and Eden, before finally losing herself to the churn of the Irish Sea. I continue south-east on long straight roads, on through Smithfield, on through Newtown. Getting a little twistier now as Cumbria regains her confidence. A bleep from the GPS at Brampton offers my first route instruction in England, pitching me into a series of fells and pikes to my right.

A rise in the gradient lifts me to the A69, then snakes, slow and steady to Milton, Kirkhouse, Hallbankgate. I am checking off towns from the way up now. Cold Fell Pike swings up above me as I sneak under Tindale, a sharp climb to Midgeholme, Halton-lea-gate, Lambley. The road clambers around Byers Pike, threading me into a hidden valley alongside the Pennine Way.

I filter south, through Slaggyford and Kirkhaugh, the road pinched in with the South Tynedale Railway by Knarsdale Forest, Grey Nag and Pike Rigg. Suddenly I'm in Raise, and from there a short hop across the river into Alston.

As I pile onto the cobbles at the bottom of Front Street, I stumble into the back wheels of other cyclists. Our pace aboard the bikes is dismissed as an irrelevance when it turns out we all walk at the same speed. We trudge up together with only the very occasional die-hard cranking past us at speeds of up to 4mph.

Exiting Alston towards Yad Moss a few moments after ten, the last three and a half kilometres of this leg lift me at an average 6% to 420m. I finally crest and drop into the control some 20 minutes later.

Wednesday 1027hrs
556 miles. Arrive Alston Southbound.

The dominant feeling in the control is relief. At this point, after all, we are two thirds of the way up the final proper hill of the event. There are barely 300 miles left in the route and nobody I speak to thinks for a second it will be anything less than possible. Horror stories of our last legs are shared and reports from prior controls filter into our conversation from the brevet desk. Officially, any 0800 starter that isn't here by now is Out Of Time, but given that the waters at Ettrick are still impassable by vehicle, the organisers graciously extend our allowance by two hours. This means little for anyone still caught north of the floods, some 68 miles back, but it seems some flexibility will be offered around 'catching up the time' before the final controls.

Glad to have pushed through the storm, I have around eight hours in hand. This gives me two whole days to get back to London. It is hard not to relax indoors, enjoying the shelter, food and company. I remove my makeshift waterproofs and settle in at the table. Everything smells wonderful, enveloped in an intricate and warming mixture of sandalwood, honey, nutmeg, clove, saffron, ginger lily. Good thoughts incubate within an ochre halo. All is well.

Twenty minutes later Rimas arrives. Standing out clearly as a grey figure against a backdrop of dazzling Sienna, his ashen features betray the differing quality of our prior night's accommodation. He looks wrecked and I am reminded just how quickly things can turn.

Eight hours is not that long. Too much has been invested in getting me here to risk a knock out by mechanical and I resolve not to eat into too much of the slack I've earned. The bike needs a little fettling. Some oil wouldn't go amiss. I thank her with a set of new zip-ties all round. Rich's has worked its way up the cleat mast and is now sitting free from the chain. Its presence is re-assuring. I leave it attached.

Wednesday 1235hrs
Targetting 600 miles.
Yad Moss and Middleton Tyas.
46 hours remaining.

The little control marking civilisation drops out of sight as I hug the gradient around a left hand corner. Onwards, into the wind, towards the peak. The clunkiness in the chain is enhanced by a worrying stiffness in the gear levers that has been developing since Eskdalemuir. I lost access to the granny[14] ring when I pushed the boom out, but with a 39/34 gear[15] available from the middle ring, I've not been missing it too much. Now, though, I don't seem to be able to reach the big rings at the back. With both hands I can just about force it onto a 39/13, which is pretty hard going for this terrain. My knees are begging me to crank the shifter a little further, but a cable snap here will mean trying to climb the remainder of Yad Moss on the hi-limit screw. This is not a plan I favour.

Tufts of grass hunker down against the gale, little flickers of silver reflect from suddenly exposed undersides as the wind beats them flat against the gradient. Solitary randonneurs recreate the scene in macrocosm, heads down into the wind, onwards and upwards.

---

14 *The smallest chain wheel on a triple crank set, giving access to very low gear ratios.*

15 *Gears allow a cyclist to vary his/her rate of travel, whilst maintaining a comfortable pedalling speed (cadence). Ratios are expressed as the number of teeth on the input cog (chainring) to those on the output cog (rear sprocket). For example, a gear ratio of 39/13 will see the wheel revolve three times for each turn of the pedals.*

As the road straightens, I begin to feel pretty exposed on the lonely hillside. There are no trees, no cars, no other cyclists. I measure my progress against scattered piles of cold rock. It's bitterly cold and I wonder if I should have put the bin bags back on before I left Alston. In this gear, stopping at the roadside is really not an option.

I'm quietly confident though. In daylight it's hard to reconcile the landscape with my frenzied descent some 30 hours earlier. The gradient is the same, but going uphill, into the wind, it's somehow easier. There's very little here, and certainly nothing I haven't ridden before. No sudden surprises. No unexpected climbs. No reason to do anything other than keep pedalling. I resolve to push a little harder, just to keep warm.

Working hard to cross the picturesque bridge at Ashgill Force, I am again comforted by the ardent aroma of the last control. I can't place the root. Sesame? Citrus? Pomegranate? It feels like climbing into a warm bed. I look around for the source, but there is little flora to generate such a spell. It stays with me on the bare roadside, climbing first to 500, then 600 metres. A cattle grid takes me from Cumbria to County Durham, and two and half miles later I hit a waypoint marking the peak of Yad Moss. The wind has been doing more to slow me than the gradient, but I am glad to know there is no more climbing.

Knowing where the cattle grids are takes the edge off the descent. I marked most as I ambled north, but the odd few that I omitted are easily recognised by the closing fences on either side of the road. As a dedicated suburbanite back home, these things are learnt on the road.

Contrasting with the downshift, the gear lever slots easily into top. I take advantage of the gradient, shedding 200m and descending rapidly through Harwood and Langdon Beck. Up ahead I can trace a view between the peaks that will drop me to North Yorkshire and my eventual destination for this leg. The Tees Valley slopes away on my right, offering an uninterrupted vista running to Meldon Hill and Mickle Fell.

A mile down the road I'm still accelerating. A tiny Methodist chapel marks the passing of Forest in Teesdale, a sign for High Force, Low Force screams past me like it's been rear-projected, added as an afterthought in post production. Another 100m lost. I try to keep it below 30mph. The boulder-strewn bed of the Tees appears in the valley below me, playing hide and seek behind my front brake lever. New Biggin screams past, I brake hard for Middleton in Teesdale and finally swing across the river to mark the end of a 25 minute descent that has carried me over 10 miles. There's a short climb on the other side, but battling to get out of top gear I have little option other than to power up on momentum. I'm still rolling fast when I cross the Lune, the road running parallel to a disused rail bridge taking ramblers along the Pennine Way.

On through Mickleton, Romaldkirk, dip and rise to Cotherstone before settling into a long and lazy climb to Lartington. The pace eases off a little and I use the increased stability to attack the gear levers with exploratory vigour. It alternates between very crunchy on the front rings to complete lock up at the rear. My guess is the cable outers are fouled. Water ingress via the upturned bar end shifters, or river crud from Scotland. Until I can fix it, I'll be running as a twin speed. 53/11 for the flats. 39/11 for the hills.

Two miles down the B2667, I find sudden distraction when Barnard Castle abruptly looms above me. On the way up, I distinctly remember this town as "left, at a roundabout". On the way back, the marketplace roundabout remains, but there is also a very evident and enormous ruin, built in aureate stone, perched atop the Tees gorge with a commanding view of every road within a good few miles.

I know from my marathon days that the first casualty to exhaustion is peripheral vision. In London 2004, this made finding the faces of my family in the crowd hard. In Barnard Castle, it has obscured an entire 12th century acropolis. As if to underline my omission, the road wraps me around three sides of its sandstone tower, never out of sight, dominating even the 14th Century Great Hall that flanks it. Still within its gaze as I pedal east out of town, I stumble directly into the landscaped gardens of the Bowes Museum.

If the castle was the jab, then the museum is the cross that floors me. The gold topped ironwork of its ornamental gates give an unexpected glimpse of Versailles. Behind the formal parterre planting, the edifice of a magnificent 19th century chateau rises. Built in the grand French style, as incongruous in scale as it is in manner. I'm left, wobbling along the tiny road to Westwick, wondering if I'm hallucinating it, or it's hallucinating me.

I'm still tugging on the gear lever through Westwick and Whorlton when I recognise the switchbacks dropping me down to the wooden bridge. I manage to crunch my way to the front middle ring in anticipation of the gradient on the other side, but find my way blocked by a bunched group of cyclists. We struggle up together as an orchestra of grunts and knee cracks.

The climb levels out as we crest over Wycliffe and our reward is evident in the flatlands ahead. The route becomes a series of straight roads linked by 90 degree turns, their spacing determined by hectare and acre rather than gradient. The regimented rhythm of agronomic division carries me through Caldwell and Forcett, climbing to Melsonby, ducking under the A1M just north of Scotch Corner and dropping into the control, on the left.

Wednesday 1643hrs
602 miles. Arrive Middeton Tyas.

Once again we gather on the outskirts of town, in the hall of the newly-built primary school. The building is slightly schizophrenic in its setting. Constructed to a modernist design in steel, brick and artificial stone, it gives the impression that it annexes a lively and progressive business community. An entry on Wikipedia has this to say about it:

"Middleton Tyas is a village and civil parish in the Richmondshire district of North Yorkshire, England... The village had a post office and shop but it closed in April 2003."

That said, the population are out in force, and they lay on an excellent service. A gratefully-received sports massage restores my legs, whilst mechanics emerge to bring life back into the 'bent's gearing. We manage together to get some reliability on the two front rings, but the rear remains adamant that top gear is the only option. After two hours' effort I have to agree, and at 7pm, I make my way back to the road.

In top.

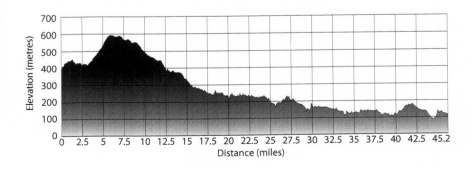

Wednesday 1902hrs
Bomber Command

A rolling start (courtesy of a diligent volunteer manning the stage) sees me back onto the road, and I immediately get lost in a series of lanes. Thus far, the GPS has been doing very well to keep me out of trouble, and the little green line I'm trailing extends some 600 miles back without more than a couple of dead ends. The problem is, I'm now trying to distinguish between the verdant thread I weaved on my way up, and the near identical twine running ahead of me to the south. Every time I pick the wrong one, the issue is compounded by another stroke added to the map. After ten minutes of near blind trial and error, Middleton Tyas looks like a spaghetti painting. I have diligently coloured in almost every road in the area to create a Gordian knot of route and track. I pull up, staring with bewilderment at the GPS as competing instructions fight for real estate on its tiny two inch screen.

I zoom out a little, see that the general direction I need is south-east, and set about chasing my shadow out of town. 20 seconds later I stumble back past the entrance to the school, gratefully tag onto the rear wheel of a departing rider, and follow him a full 100 metres down the road to our first route point.

I am clearly more tired than I thought, and all this stop-starting in top is not helping. We wind down the hillside, east out of town, then swing south into gently undulating countryside. The middle ring isn't particularly keen to hold onto the chain, so I'm pushing along in top. Cruising flat lanes at 22mph, I soon drop my rescuer. The road kinks a little to break up the distance. Through Moulton, Uckerby, long way round The Green at Scorton. An eight mile stretch without instruction takes me through Bolton-on-swale, Ellerton and Kiplin. The hills of the North York Moors National Park come into view ahead, and with fear I know I'll touch them before I pull into Coxwold.

As I catch sight of the river at Great Langton, I recognise a tail light up ahead and find myself catching Rimas. We ride together in the fading light, out and around Sweden Sykes, through Yafforth, over the A684 into Warlaby. I'm surprised to find him ahead of me, but know I lost a fair amount of time resting up at the last control. "Have you stopped?" I ask.

"Not much time"

Its 8pm now. He's been up since four, got maybe two hours' sleep the night before, and has ridden through the day.

"Have you slept?"

"On Yad Moss. Pretty fast."

"You OK?"

"Woke up with front wheel on grass. Stopped before wall."

That was a 30mph descent, over cattle grids, in the middle of the day. Waking up with the handlebars under your palms is scary enough. Doing it on a major gradient through very remote terrain must have been horrendous.

"You OK now?"

"Am OK."

For the early starters, Coxwold closes just before sundown. I figure he's got about an hour to close 15 miles. He's moving at maybe 10.

We ride together through Newby Wiske, but I'm finding it hard going at this speed when the way ahead gets bumpy. The general trend has been downhill, but eight miles in we've bottomed out and the route ahead is peppered with short and sharp 15m climbs. Powering up in top on these legs means hitting each rise at a minimum 20mph. At half of that, the cadence is going to destroy me. We cross the Wiske together on the approach to South Otterington, but the rollers on the A167 soon see Rimas lost to my rear mirror.

On through Newsham, trace my way back over the railway, then idle out alongside Thirsk Racecourse. As the sky begins to darken, I catch another glimpse of hills ahead. Closer now.

The road onward takes me through the North Yorkshire equivalent of suburbia. Thirsk and Sowerby join hands in an uninterrupted chain of houses. As Sowerby Road gives way to Front Street, I find myself in a wide tree-lined avenue. It's an estate agent's dream. Mature trees shelter grassy islands flanking both sides of the road. The canopy catches the last of the sunlight, basking me in a warm chromatic glow, some 35 metres wide. Ahead, long shadows run from my front wheel, stretching out to the horizon before being slowly consumed by the cold burn of my front light.

Under the A168 and I'm edging fields again. The going gets hilly as I approach Little Thurkleby and settle into the last half hour of this leg. I'm climbing steadily, trying to keep the pressure on the pedals. My right knee has developed a nasty creak and I'm battling to keep the 'bent moving forwards at anything less than 15mph. Still battle-damaged from Eskdalemuir, the 'bent and I are locked in desperate partnership. She needs me to get her home. I need her to get me there. The brake lines are crusted up. The gears don't work. We're climbing low over the English countryside and I begin to feel like the pilot of a Lancaster bomber, on a desperate run home. In dire need of support, I send an update to my loved ones:

"Cockpit shot to sh1t, rear derailleur stuck in top, gremlins in the cables, starboard engine on fire. Coming in low and fast over North York Moors. Clear the decks!!!"

I'm tugging uselessly on the gear levers, but can't get out of top. I know this stage ends with a big climb. I've got to build speed. Hit it fast. Trees close over the road again and I push through the darkness, swooping up to 95m. The control is on the top of a hill. I crest at 16mph, knees screaming, but there's only darkness. As the road pitches downward I can see it runs out with a sharp rise on the other side of a small valley. Need more speed. I start a second dive. 19mph. 20. 21. Pedalling hard now, counting pedal strokes. A church with an octagonal tower blips past on the right. I recognise it too late. This is Coxwold! I look up. A man stands in the road, waving me in with a torch. I'm less than 10 metres from him and closing fast. I have just enough breath left to give a warning yell.

A second later, the 'bent and I slide sideways under his outstretched arm, just about keeping the bike upright as the road kicks and buckles for grip underneath. As we come to a halt, the GPS flashes up 'CTRL R'.

Wednesday 2120hrs
Arrive Coxwold Southbound. 635 miles.
Hours in the bag: 5 and a half.

I lean the 'bent up around the back of the control, and head inside to collect the obligatory proof of passage. The continued pace has transformed Coxwold beyond recognition. On Monday afternoon cyclists milled around the car park, taking a little rest for the route ahead. Indoors the bubble of easy conversation flowed bountifully over sunlit tables, nervous energy surfacing in garrulous oration. I struggled to bring myself to leave. It's Wednesday evening now and the focus is solely 'stamp, fettle, fuel, go'. Schedule dictates I get back to Thorne before my final sleep.

Do this, and tomorrow will bring the finish within a 180 mile day. Fail, and its closer to 250.

I cannot do another 24 hour ride at this point.

All of this noted, it's cold outside, and the volunteers at Coxwold are making lasagne. Fresh batch in six minutes. I can wait.

I fill my time squatting by torchlight outside the door, eyeing up the rear mech. Worryingly, the derailleur moves just fine, but the cable remains locked tight. If I can't get inside to clean it, I'll be needing a new cable and outer. Of course, its routed internally through the frame, so will not be a trivial fix. I manage to free the brakes a little, which restores some semblance of safety. Crud in the cables. My ongoing ministrations attract the assistance of a volunteer, who begins a series of diagnostics on the bike. A call comes out from the kitchen and I am ushered back inside.

I allow myself a forty minute turnaround. Reviewing the route indoors, I can see I'm almost home. OK, I'm still north of York, but significantly, I'm back on the east side of England. No more crossing the middle, no more crazy climbs, no more fells, bens, lochs, pikes, glens. Maybe one vale, but that's flat. This is good. It's an almost direct line south from here to London and I have barely 400km to go.

I return to the bike a half hour later. Fresh water in the camelbak. Banana sitting atop lasagne. Fuel that will close the 60 miles to Thorne. Its dark, but in range.

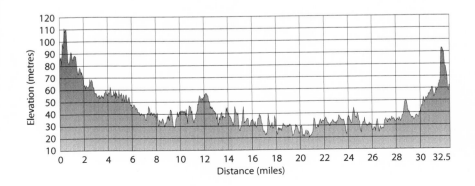

Wednesday 2213hrs
Depart Coxwold. Bed in 60 miles. 37 hours left.

No joy with the cables, so it's a very slow start as I unwind myself from three sides of the building before exiting back to the crossroads. Once on the open road I know I will only have a short sprint before the climbs get underway. I'm pushing hard to make the most of this tiny flat.

Left at the cross and the Howardian rollercoaster begins. Down to the bottom of the village, up and over in darkness, dip into Newburgh Grange, accelerating hard. Long climb now, past the priory, away from the warmth of town, tired muscles digging hard into the hillside. 70m above, 80, 100, 140, 148, 150. I crest under trees, blind to the view ahead.

Pass Oulston on the drop, lose the moon as I fall, but keep the speed, pushing on into the shadows, always swelling, up and down. The road writhes left and right but I stay with her, clattering towards the double summit at Crayke. Back down in the 70s now, 80, 90, 107. That's the first. 90. 100, 105, 110 and I'm done. Down and out, braking hard for the T Junction, then a long run out into the Vale of York.

The moon is restored. Long flat roads take me through Stillington, Strensall, Towthorpe. It's dark out here. 90 degree turns steal rear lights from sight. The cold bites into my legs, slips under the waistband of my windproof, edges along my wrists. Silvery fingers trying to take hold of my core. I begin to feel very vulnerable. I miss the high hedges of Kent, cocooning my training rides from the wind and the unknown. The road out here is bordered only by darkness, heather moorlands extending to my left, black fields that run right up to the roadside. A lonely streetlamp offers a shallow pool of light, and

I dive in, seeking reassurance. Rather than warm me, I am instead reminded of the opaque shadows that crowd its frail little arc. I lean forwards and angle the Cyo up, but this only gives me a better view of the void.

The route onward becomes a slightly panicked run from lamp to lamp. I will myself not to think of 'An American Werewolf in London' and in doing so, fail utterly. A zip-tie snaps and I spend a few minutes in total isolation, fumbling in the middle of an unlit road. Cold sweat clamps my movements. I can hear my heartbeat...

After three minutes I have not been eaten. A group of randonneurs swings into sight and soars past, freewheels chattering like crickets. At the back, what looks like forumite Darth Stuart's Ratcatcher. Eager to avoid being left in the dark, I quickly patch up the chainline and give chase.

They have maybe an eight minute headstart. As I begin to put in some serious effort, I find myself again washed over by the sweet scent of Ashgill. No, deeper than that... Alston. My subconscious is whirring, legs doing the thinking. Where have I smelt this? Fruits. Citrus. Not so much the aroma that's distinctive, as the warm feeling of contentment it conjures. Deep in the middle of this dark, dark, night, I find myself transported to a sunny August day. The heady sweetness of cider, spilt from glasses raised in friendly salute. Ice-chilled pools evaporating from the unpolished wood of coarse pub furniture, baked dry by a high sun.

I can almost hear the glasses chime as they bump together. But no. Something else. Deeper still. They're not glasses. Fishing floats? No. Jam jars, chinking together, in a bath-tub. Where have I seen this?

Eskdalemuir. Suddenly, it comes back to me. A memory in third person perspective. Our host for the night apologising about her bathroom. The tub decommissioned by floating jam jars. Soaking off the labels. Re-using the little glass pots to bottle massage oils. She made her own.

...And the padded table I used as a bed was their theatre. In those few blissful hours, whilst I grabbed some much needed sleep, my body restored itself, drawing flavours from the foam, absorbing their scent. Skin once macerated by the storm now lovingly wrapped in essential oils. Every time I build up a sweat, out wicks some more. As the night turns to drizzle, I realise I am not only scented. I am waterproof.

I am still laughing as I pass through Warthill, up onto a little ridge at Holtby, and earn a very brief dash along what feels like a proper road. Defined borders tame the moors and my new found confidence carries me off to the east, through the darkness to Dunnington, Elvington, chasing tail lights over the river and into the East Riding of Yorkshire.

Midway towards Sutton upon Derwent, I finally catch the group in front, introducing myself to the recumbent back-marker, Patrick. He's on fine form, but the war between schedule and sleep has left him a little wobbly. I figure it's about half twelve now, and rough calculations at the last control suggest we've probably got another two hours to go. If it was hard to measure progress on these roads by day, it's almost impossible by night. We ride together for company. For encouragement. For protection.

The pack are suffering mechanicals and pull up under a lamp post marking a right turn. I'm still stuck in top and have to choose between riding on alone, or stopping at the roadside knowing my only exit is via a 53/11 gear. I give a few exploratory pedal strokes, but the black void of the road ahead threatens to suck me in.

I decide that if the spirit of audax is self sufficiency, it needs a footnote to say, "best served in groups". I spend the next few minutes scribing loops onto the tarmac, chasing the Cyo's little orb back and forth at 2mph. It is a good test of balance. When we resume, there are five lights driving back the cavity. We pedal in unison for the next ten miles. Distances measured relative to each other. In the small hours we come across a group of Americans, clustered together under the light of a substation. It is reassuring to think of these pockets of riders, dotted along the route. They keep their own pace as we bump onwards over the level crossing at Howden, but there is never more than 500 metres between us for the rest of the leg.

The darkness retreats as we approach the Ouse at Boothferry. The artefacts of humanity begin to spill across the landscape once more. We cross the river on a 1920s swing bridge, steel girders breaking the moonlight into Morse code. Downstream to our left we can pick out the silhouette of an even greater structure, concrete spans lifting a mile of the M62 some 30 metres above the river. Man is king once again. Although we take the smallest road from the roundabout on the south bank, I know that I'm no longer scared of the dark.

As we approach Airmyn, Patrick's rear light betrays a kink in his trail. I drop back momentarily, assuming he is repositioning in his seat. The pattern repeats a couple of times, and then ever so smoothly, he drifts towards the left hand side of the road, connects with the grassy verge, and bails onto his side. He goes down without a noise, without even a break in his cadence. We pull up around him, front markers looping back, but he's already getting up.

"Fell asleep".

We regroup and set off again. Tiredness masks the distance. The roads here are a little big for navigating like this. Back along the Aire, through Rawcliffe, under the motorway, across the canal, out of East Riding and into Doncaster. When we reach the level crossing at Moorends, I know we are almost there. A mile later, playing grounds appear on our right. Follow them, right, right, right again, Thorne Rugby Club.

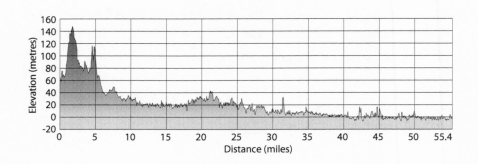

LEL DAY 5: THURSDAY

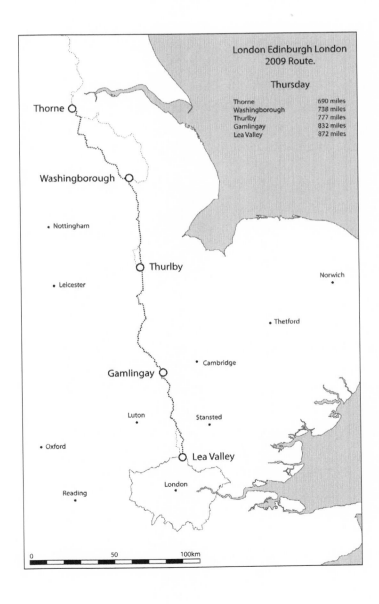

London Edinburgh London
2009 Route.

Thursday

Thorne	690 miles
Washingborough	738 miles
Thurlby	777 miles
Gamlingay	832 miles
Lea Valley	872 miles

Thorne

Washingborough

• Nottingham

Thurlby

Norwich
•

• Leicester

• Thetford

• Cambridge

Gamlingay

Luton
•

Stansted
•

• Oxford

Lea Valley

London
•

Reading
•

0   50   100km

Thursday 0301hrs
Arrive Thorne Control.
Miles travelled: 690. Miles to go: 186. Sleep.

I park up against the railings, grab the water bladder from my bag, unwrap the brevet card and stumble indoors. Things are OK. I've ridden over 190 miles since leaving Eskdalemuir and am now ready for a good sleep. If I can do again tomorrow what I've done today, I should finish in time.

First I need fuel. My brain has been resisting the maths, but I force it through anyway. It takes me an hour to work this out:

Lea Valley checkpoint closes at 1040am Friday...

(Eat some food).

190 miles today has taken me almost 24 hours...

(Try to pour a drink. Use both hands. Still miss).

I have the same distance to go.

(Wander back outside. Check zip-ties).

I need to keep at least four hours' slack in case things go awry.

(Amble back inside... Start looking for a bit of floor).

I need to be out of here whilst there are still 28 hours to go.

(Slump towards carpet. Do NOT close eyes).

10:40am Friday, minus 28 hours (count backwards on fingers)... 06:40am Thursday.

(Can I inflate my camelbak to use as a pillow?)

Knock 40 minutes off to grab some breakfast...

I need to wake up at six.

I turn on the Blackberry to set an alarm and find it's already gone four. Necessity trumps commitment. I set it for seven.

Thursday 0700hrs
Homeward Bound.

This is it then. My final day. The first thing I see is the phone's snooze button, dancing in and out of focus in a seductive waltz of amelioration. I resist her charms, knowing I've already traded an hour from the schedule. Trying not to think too much, I unwrap limbs and haul myself outdoors.

The sun has a two hour headstart on me but hasn't used the time to much effect. Riders stumble around in the grey light, with the odd gait of those who spend a lot of time at sea. I'm not quite awake. Eyes are operating in low polygon mode. Nobody seems to be casting shadows. Five deep breaths. Go get breakfast. Word indoors is the meteorologists aren't done with us yet. The MET office has issued a Severe Weather Warning for the entire east side of England. The casualty report of yesterday runs at 64 abandons, with still more missing in action. We're going to be in the thick of it again.

Honestly though. This is England. Verdant pastures. A green and pleasant land. Even when it's bad, it's little more than inclement. Scotland has recalibrated my tolerances, inuring me against foul weather and permanently waterproofing my spirits. I'm nearly home. It'll be fine. Get back to the bike. Next time that sun rises, I'm done.

As I pour myself on to the seat, I am grateful for the supine layout of the 'bent. All around me, DF riders perform a delicate ballet of contact points, trying to pull away whilst simultaneously keeping weight off handlebar, saddle and pedals. As I move to join them, it rapidly becomes obvious that the losses in ergonomics have been traded for huge gains from physics. Press-ganging the mass of the earth into the war against inertia, they stand straight legged, letting gravity pull their weight down through the pedals. Horizontal, I have no such luxury, and at 0737 I perform a knees-only exit, wobbling unconvincingly forward, still wedged in top.

A few minutes from the car park, I am pretty much up to speed. I find myself approaching a stationary rider, held motionless at a junction, arms stretched out like a scarecrow. I drift to a halt alongside and ask if he's OK. He doesn't turn toward me, and I begin to dread some Stephen King style reveal. Seems I get jumpy when I'm sleep deprived. In broken English, he explains he's lost a page from his routesheet and is trying to retrace his steps southward over the next 50 miles from memory. Paranoia aside, this is not a good thing. Firstly, we're at the first instruction on a 30 line page. Second, we're not going back via Wragby, so 90% of the next leg is going to be new ground. I explain as best I can, and am granted a simple utterance in return.

"I follow you."

Seems to be a statement of intent rather than a request, but fair on, these roads are flat and featureless. A little company will make life easier. We head off together, crossing the railway, then the canal. The landscape remains unchanged as Yorkshire's East Riding first gives way to Doncaster, then North Lincolnshire. On the approach to Sandtoft, we swing right into territories new, due south on a road so straight that we're in Nottinghamshire by the time we make a turn.

Approaching Notttinghamshire, southbound

The promised rain is holding off, but the wind sits heavily against our chests, pulling at our shoulders, pushing against us in a constant wall of enervation. Without tree, turn or town to vary the strain, it's hard going just to keep the pedals turning. All the way, my silent companion sits ten inches from my back wheel. I'm pretty sure that two bikes travel faster than one, but it sure would be nice if he'd take a turn at the front for a while.

Or just speak.

Doesn't even have to be English.

I know I'm running out of sugar when resentment begins to build. Why won't he go in front? The road doesn't even have any turnings for the next two miles. Even then, it's a SO:X. I pull towards the verge, motioning him around me. He slows, still on my back wheel, and waits. I stop.

OK. Time to raid the stores. I take a few good mouthfuls of water and wash down an energy gel. Take off the windproof. Stretch my legs. He's going to follow me all the way. Might as well get on with it.

Back on the bike, waddle it up to speed, then hook into the pedals. Push hard to keep momentum, swing south over the Idle, through Misterton and over the canal as we exit. Passing under the railway, I spy a handful of riders up ahead, air pressure binding them into tight pelotons. Walkeringhim, Beckingham, we pass each little group, but the wheelsucker stays with me.

We leave via a roundabout on the A631, joining the dual carriageway to approach Gainsborough. By the time we cross the Trent into Lincolnshire proper, we are resplendent in haulage and motorway style crash barriers. We get our first dose of rain as we climb Foxby Hill out of town, slowly building as we tick off Somerby, Upton, Kexby, Willingham, Stow, Sturton.

Another long straight drag extends south-east over the Till, tipping upwards at the end to reveal riders waiting to turn right along Lincoln Cliff towards North Carlton. Tucking in behind, we are rewarded with a view that extends back into Nottinghamshire. 60 metres up, over this kind of range, I can clearly see the weather system gathering strength. As we continue south towards Burton and over the A46, the heavens begin to open.

The steep descent into Lincoln sees our rising pace matched by an equivalent increase in the ferocity of the weather. We're in full-on cloud burst by the time we reach edge of town. I'm feathering the brakes as I go, pulling back on the levers when either wheel has traction, easing off whenever we start to drift. Peaking 23mph, I follow the GPS and routesheet into Yarborough Road, and am suddenly confronted by industrial-size kitchen bins blocking the route ahead. I brake heavy and claim the gentlest of nudges from the rear. Suffice to say that by the time I've scrambled a three pointer, my mute shadow is giving me a little more space on the road.

Lincoln city centre has diversion signs out. He and I spend the next few minutes taking exploratory stabs into cul-de-sacs of varying depth. Having collected a wet cyclist from each dead end, we eventually reach a critical mass where the wisdom of crowds comes into effect. Tendrils of the group slowly unravel towards the high street. We're now moving at a far more pedestrian pace and our rising numbers are gathering attention from the roadside.

"Why would you go for a ride TODAY?" (Hmmm... How to explain this? Technically, we went for a ride on Sunday...)

"Where are you going?" (The most credible answer seems to be Washingborough. We tried 'London', but people didn't believe us.)

"Is it a race?" (I'm assuming they've spotted the numbers taped to our frames, as our pace is less than expeditious.)

We leave the heavier rain in Lincoln, heading due south on a very industrial-looking Broadgate. Its dual carriageways take us over Pelham Bridge, the motor traffic increasing in velocity and frequency as the road widens. The raised pace better suits my gearing, but the weight of traffic is becoming nothing short of frightening. Fenced in by guardrails and 'get in lane' signs, there is little option to reconsider, until, just when I decide its clearly all gone wrong, the pack swings left onto a quiet lane, towards Canwick.

The change is instant. Traffic noise mutes immediately. The pace slows. Bird song. We idle along the hillside above the cemetery, claiming our first proper view of the imposing medieval cathedral, rising across the valley over Lincoln. As we descend under the railway, a scattering of houses spring up on our right. Less than a mile later, reversed by our new approach, the control appears on our left.

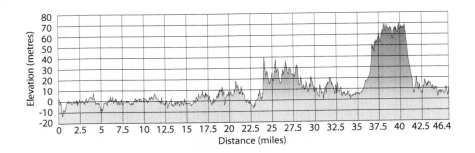

Thursday 1105hrs
Arrive Washingborough.
23hrs 35minutes left, and 137 miles to go.
Still stuck in top...

There's a fair amount of duck and cover going on in the control. The capricious distribution of sunshine and monsoon has left the pack dominated by rumour and superstition. All eyes are on the windows as the landscape outside is alternately baked and drenched by the whims of weather. The viciousness of the deluge is tempered only by its tight focus, and each batch of arriving randonneurs demonstrate an inverse bell-curve of bone dry or sodden. One brave soul sleeps outside on a bench, whilst other side of the building rattles under the downpour.

Departing riders gather against the glass, trying to gauge their exit to avoid the frequent stripes of heavy rain. As I approach the brevet desk, I hear my wheelsucker chance his routine on another of our number. I duck out of sight, wondering if he's been doing this all the way...

Thursday 1157hrs
Depart Washingborough. Targeting Thurlby.

The sun is reflecting brightly off the still-wet tarmac as I leave on roads now recognisable from the way up. I'm back on the main drag and making good time. The route south from here will toy with the eastern edge of the Lincoln escarpment, rolling us up and down the limestone ridge, scribing a sine wave of some 30m amplitude into my GPS. The terrain suits my gearing and mood perfectly, push hard, gather speed, blast down, hit the next one still rolling.

My lightweight windproof jacket does little to keep out the rain so I've stashed it in my seat pack along with my gloves. This leaves me with a thin baselayer worn over the short-sleeved commemorative LEL jersey and a buff. This is my preferred costume for day rides. Its reasonably cool in direct sun, acts like a wet-suit in pouring rain and dries rapidly whilst still in place. What's left in the ride, after all, is little more than a day's effort. I'll put the extra layers back on if it gets cold after nightfall.

Just as I start to climb into Branston, the storm comes back in force. Looks like I've timed this all wrong. Thick and greasy raindrops hurl themselves into the floor around me. A mad percussionist in the cloud above bends pavement into snare drums, cars into a steel pan orchestra.

Waiting at the crossroads at the top of town, I can see heavier clouds coming in from the north, dragging rains across the junction directly in front of me with the clatter of dropped cutlery. The temperature drops a few degrees and the hail begins. Stretched out on the 'bent, I'm a tempting target for the avalanche and have to quickly manoeuvre myself under the protective portico of a handy Euronics store.

I'm barely tucked in, my right arm is drenched, but at least it doesn't hurt any more. The tiny white exocets bounce comically onto my chest, unable to hit me with any force. I stay here for three minutes. A wall of freezing rain marks the tail end of the storm fringe and I realise that if I'm going to outrun this thing I need to get ahead of it. I don't wait for the rain to stop before pulling out and giving chase.

The landscape opens up as I clamber up towards Metheringham. I'm pushing hard at 17mph and can clearly see the maelstrom edging along the steep western scarp of Lincoln Cliff a mile or so to my right. The road ahead will take me south for another couple of miles before swinging me directly across its path. Passing Blankney, we're about neck and neck, but as I plunge through Scopwick the winds are already starting to whistle around me.

I begin to appreciate why the geography curriculum commits so much time to the architecture of weather and so little to learning where things actually are. Cars, and to some degree my GPS, have reduced navigation to simple fuelling choices, but knowing what that storm will be doing ten minutes from now could change everything. Five miles under those clouds will take more effort than forty in the dry.

I'm blinded by glacial rain on the approach to Digby but daren't slow down. Pushing on into the wall of hail, the storm swallows me once again. Crosswinds batter me. Twisting updrafts drive freezing water into my skin. I'm laid back, taking most of it on my chest and thighs. A two inch puddle has formed in my seat. A primal scream drives me onward.

I push on as fast as I dare, head tucked into my chest against the hail. I've got the buff pulled up tight under my eyes and am trying to exhale downward to keep my glasses from fogging. The exertion is making it hard going and I'm frequently losing sight of the kerb to my left. Deciding that the overhang of my helmet will protect my eyes from the worst of it, I tuck my glasses into my shirt instead.

Just past Dorrington I finally graduate into warm rains and from there into sunshine once more. The dark amaranthine threat above shrinks in my mirror, finally losing ground behind me. I speed on to Ruskington, pushing hard to extend my lead as the road takes me east through the town. I want some space between me and another dose. I've been on the road for an hour and have already been drenched twice.

On momentary high ground I can see the road ahead curving lazily around Leasingham Moor, taking me west into Sleaford. I'll lose time cutting across country and am likely to pick up a third soaking before this one dries off. Surfing the front of the storm is going to see me repeatedly dunked but I've no idea how far back the storm reaches. If I wait for it to pass, I could lose hours. Besides the underpass of the A17, there's no protection to hide me anyway. No. The next control is probably no further than 25 miles away. I can get there and either skip on or sit it out with some food and company. It's not that bad.

Just as I've resolved to keep going, I'm brought to a sudden halt by an explosive burning in my right eye. Bug strike! A direct hit at 28mph. I lose a few minutes at the side of the road, squatted down, waiting, eye folded tight against the pain. Should have put my glasses back on. Stupid. Stupid. Stupid.

The pain doesn't recede. My rocking figure attracts the help of a rambling couple, who kindly dab at me with tissues. My eye is streaming effusively, but they can find no evidence of the bug, nor shrapnel from its tiny body. I resolve that the burning is probably more the result of ingress by massage oil, and crack open the seat pack to get my medi-pack and swabs. Although the aeropod is sold as water resistant, it clearly wasn't expecting things to be this wet and I find I've been carrying a puddle with me for the last few days. The first item I remove from its depths is a travel pack of tissue which has been melded by the rain into a giant stogie of cold wet paper. To be honest, this is pretty much ideal and I keep it held against my eye for a few more minutes whilst I locate the saline pipette.

After waving a handful of randonneurs past I make my way back to the road. Again I'm indebted to my wife for purchasing (and insisting I bring) the first aid kit.

Rimas sails past on the descent and I give chase. My eye is still burning so I pop the right lens out of my glasses and allow the drizzle to cool it. This has hidden benefits, as not only am I now entirely fog proof on the remaining lens, I also have one eye for drizzle, and one for hail.

I push on to through Sleaford, over the level crossing, and am embraced by the storm once again. I recognise the pattern as the road swings right, breaching concentric walls of freezing rain, hail, and spray. This time its cooling effect is entirely welcomed and I push through without complaint. I emerge on the road south to Stow, chasing a tandem couple up and down over the bumps.

I catch them on the outskirts of the village and spend the next few miles in very pleasant company. Turns out they hail from Costa Rica but their UK base is on my daily commute. We're pretty much matched for speed over this terrain so have plenty of time to agree we're all about to get drenched again. I stay with them until just after 2pm.

Rounding the corner towards Aslackby, I start to hallucinate tiny figures in the verge ahead. Not sure if it's exhaustion, rain playing havoc with my vision, or some bizarre after effect of the bug strike, but I'd swear there are pixies lining the right hand side of the road. As I get closer to the junction I can clearly make out impish faces tucked under bright coloured caps. There're maybe five of them, beady little eyes watching me, each figure ranging between eight and sixteen inches tall. They're actually quite realistic looking...

As I slow up to wipe some of the rain out of my eyes, I realise that there is a hidden trench running under the tree coverage on my right. Laid up within it with, only their heads visible through the grass, is a small platoon of riders. Better than that, I recognise the front and rear markers as Gerry and Brian. They invite me into their makeshift shelter and I gratefully accept.

I am introduced to Greenbank and Xavier and we happily pass ten minutes speculating over the weather, watching the rains build again, waving at the Costa Ricans as they diligently plough past. Gerry very kindly offers me his jacket, but the thought of putting dry over wet seems pointless. We opt instead to celebrate with a photograph.

Sitting (Front to back): Greenbank, Xavier, Unknown Rider, Brian.
Standing: Me.

Photo: GerryC

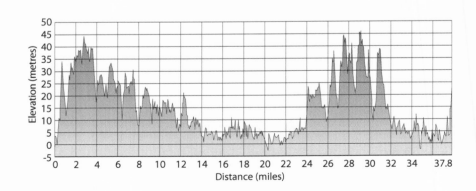

Thursday 1422hrs
Diversionary tactics

From our verge-side camp all seem pretty confident the storm will move west. The feeling in the group is that we should wait here for the worst of it to pass, then tuck in behind and nip down the 'alternate' route of the A15 to Thurlby. It's nine rather than twelve miles and is a significantly faster road. Best of all, it stays due south and will keep a few miles between us and the projected path of the rain.

This is my first audax and I'm not entirely sure that what we're about to do is within the rules. I hang back as the group set off, looking to Brian for advice. My dithering nearly dismounts a few of us and turns out to be entirely wasted when Brian announces he's taking the A15 too. Good enough for him is good enough for me. Not in top gear at 5mph though... I push hard and get rolling. We part with the received route at a crossroads and an infectious mood moves through the group. The sun is out, the surface smooth. I begin to feel like a truant schoolboy, errantly bunking double geography.

We turn due south, get a little dip and then plough straight into a climb. There's a long crest but I can see the pattern repeats ahead at least twice more. Consistent with every hill since Yad Moss, my compulsory gear choice demands I hit each summit at a fair lick. The traffic is fast moving and this is not the place for a wobbly ascent. We're travelling at about 20mph on the downs, maybe 12 on the ups, but my forced cadence is going to kill my knees if I try to climb at less than 15. I need to take advantage of the gradient whilst it's still in my favour.

Of course I can't just break away, as my navigation has been reduced to following a rear wheel, off-piste on a route sheet that relies on dead reckoning. As we begin the next dip, I ask the wheel's owner for confirmation of the route ahead. The call comes back "Just head down 20 miles or so, then swing right!!!"

Seems simple enough. I push ahead, and shoot past the front marker doing about twice his speed. By the next summit, they're gone from my mirrors, lost on the other side of the hill. I'm treated to a solo climb around some woodland, then the ground begins to level out. The road curves right to pass between Hanthorpe and Morton, past Cawthorpe still moving fast.

I take advantage of a section of flat road to pull up the waypoint marking the next control on the GPS. With some surprise, I note that it's less than 10 miles away. I'm moving faster than I thought.

20 seconds later, I hit the outskirts of Bourne. The diversion loses a few cleverness points when I discover the main road through town is being dug up. With the traffic slowed to near standstill, I edge gingerly through the queues, determined not to get stranded here in top. I spend five minutes happily trailing a white people carrier, claiming waves from the occupants of the rear seats.

As I clear the roundabout marking the southmost extent of town, the rollers begin again. I get another short climb, resolving in a nice descent through Northorpe. I'm leaning in hard for the countering swell when the GPS sends me right on a tiny residential road that I recognise from the way up. Last time I was here I was chasing the sag wagon. Now I'm 780 miles into my ride and only a hundred miles from home.

I'm going to make it.

I greet a few cyclists as they depart the control, all of whom are most surprised that I'm facing the wrong way.

Thursday 1502 hrs
Arrive Thurlby Control.
20 hours left. 96 miles to go.

An unknown bystander waiting outside the primary school does a double take when I roll past stretched out all horizontal. I guess they don't have many recumbent shops up this way when he asks, "You made it?"

I get this question a lot on my commute, but it's far more common on my other 'bent. I'll concede that most laid back bikes have more than a little of the Heath Robinson about them, but this one hardly looks home brew. I am, after all, sitting atop what is pretty much state of the art engineering: a lightweight single piece butted split tube aluminium frame, air-shock suspended and tricked out with a seat, boom and crankset knitted from dinosaurs. This is a serious bit of kit, and after all we've shared, I feel quite protective of her.

"No, it's a Challenge Furai SL-II," I manage to splutter in defence, whilst he chuckles at my evident exasperation.

"No... You made it *round*."

Ah... Slight embarrassment. To be fair, he has probably had quite a lot more sleep than me, and it was dark last time we met. This is the tech who got me rolling with the cleat plate on Sunday night. I owe him my event. I park up and eagerly give him the 20 second version of adventures shared since departing northbound. He ushers me indoors towards food and rest and I quickly find myself surrounded with familiar faces from the last few legs. It looks like we're in sync now and I've finally found my pace group. The Costa Ricans are here.

Rimas is stumbling around sleeplessly. Gerry, Greenbank and Xavier roll in together not long after, bashfully confessing their directions may not have been entirely to scale. They appear quite relieved I made the turn.

Gerry displays enviable control of his body by first checking it's OK with the others, then falling asleep instantly. The ambulant remainder sit down to join me as I finish my food. Conversations suggest they might spend a couple of hours here before heading on. Refuelled and rested, I'm eager to take on the few miles that are left, even if it means setting off on my own. The rains seem to be settling down outside, and I resolve to claim the next bit of sunshine for my departure.

I hook up with Brian in the foyer on my way out. His bike is inverted, rear wheel all skewed, tracking like a second-hand VHS tape. Techs inspect spokes, rim and tyre, fingers swarming over buckled surfaces like insects on a tin of syrup. The quality of care we riders receive is nothing short of exemplary, especially considering that the organisers made no promise of mechanical assistance. Everyone here is volunteering their time and expertise for free.

My already high thoughts are further compounded when I return outside and find that for the first time in over 200 miles I have a full choice of gears on the rear cassette. My rescuer waves me off with a grin and the pear drop smell of fresh WD40.

Thursday 1646hrs
Ever Southwards.

Back on the A15 towards Baston, this feels more like a victory lap than a last desperate stand. There's a fair amount of mind play to riding long distance and my normal strategy in the closing quarter is to discard the cumulative miles. Facing incomprehensible distance, I treat the final leg as a standalone venture. In training rides, this would see me 190 miles in, desperately floundering against a target 250. Discard the log. You're 60 miles from home. Simple distance. Ride it.

As I head south of Thurlby, I'm having the opposite issue. I'm 90 percent done and with the prior 780 miles branded viscerally on my brain, cannot help but see the remaining hundred as a mere triviality. I know I'm underestimating things, but I just cannot take it seriously.

Heading into open countryside, the landscape is tamed into gentle risers. The surface is smooth. There are road markings, even. I leave the A15 at Kate's Bridge, following the canal south to the horizon. With the exception of a small kink at West Deeping, the road is almost perfectly straight. Without turn or feature to distract me, I can finally force myself to acknowledge the task at hand. Yes, there are 'only' a hundred miles left, but setting off for a hundred miler at 5pm is always going to be a serious undertaking. Especially if you've only had two and half hours' sleep, and have already spent ten hours on the bike today.

On the plus side, it looks like it'll be plain sailing. The storm is erased from mirror and mind by the time that same road carries me into Peterborough. The sun is high on my right shoulder, floating in an uninterrupted sky that is at least twice the size of anything I've seen in my native Kent. Without ridge, cliff or knoll to stir up the heavens, I can expect a very pleasant four hours of balmy evening ahead.

Not far past Lolham, two railway crossings and the march of pylons across my path provide the unmistakeable evidence of a return to inhabited territories. A short climb lifts me towards Upton, gently feeding the road through a small series of hills before lowering me to the Cambridgeshire borders. With the luxury of gears, the inclines pass un-noted.

Emerging to turn west above the Nene, I am whipped up to speed by heavy traffic on the A47. Although only a single carriageway at this point, it feels (and is driven) like a much bigger road. There are lay-bys and everything. Ahead of me, the ongoing route climbs to a fairly busy looking roundabout with what is very probably the A1.

Scrolling up-screen on the GPS, I watch the dotted line swing south again in about a mile. To my eye, this is the same distance as that roundabout, at which I seem to have an E01. Panning back down, I note a small service road on my left combines with the 90 degree exit ahead to make a right angled triangle. One too many cups of tea in Thurlby means I am in fairly dire need of a comfort break anyway, so I take the opportunity to cut the corner. Not only do I get to avoid the junction, I'm also raising my chances of finding a discrete bush.

A gently sloping bank drops away to the river. A row of silent vehicles warms slowly in the sun. I resolve to push past the elevated cabs of the sleeping HGVs, trusting provenance to deliver more privacy further from the main drag. I spin out a few hundred metres short of Wansford, my planned route neatly bisected by the Great North Road. This was not the plan.

With no more road ahead, and the river barring my route south, there's nothing else for it but to retrace my steps. I cruise slowly along the ceaseless array of vehicles lining the verge, wondering whether this is an innocent rest stop or the dogging capital of The East. Necessity builds, and finding a gap where the rooflines of the cars are a little lower, I take the opportunity to park up, shuffle down the bank, and hopefully remove myself from sight.

The requisite arrangements are complicated by my wearing cycle shorts under my usual longs, and on inspection, the rain soaked fabric is clearly beginning to rub. Three days of perpetually damp layering threaten to make the remaining miles very uncomfortable, and with a nod to Rich's fate at Coxwold, I opt to remove the offending articles as soon as possible. I slide a little further towards the riverfront. If this isn't just a lay-by, I don't want to get pulled up for false advertising.

Up at the roadside, my bike is beginning to attract attention. Two men are looking over it, and I can't tell from here whether their interest is appreciative or covetous. With eyes firmly on the 'bent, I quickly change out of my shorts, knowing there's very little I can do in my intermediate state if either decides to suddenly lift it into a vehicle. As it turns out, my more immediate issue is the family aboard the narrowboat, hushed engine announcing its arrival all of twenty feet from me. With nothing between me and the Nene, I suspect they get a more corporeal view than might be reasonably billed. With one and a half legs in my longs, I do a quick rendition of the hopping man before falling headlong up the bank, scurrying back to my bike, and departing to a chorus of whoops and jeers.

With distance, decency and comfort restored, it's a sunny and pleasant afternoon. I track back to the main road and climb up to the first, and pivotally *second* roundabouts. First exit at number one carries me safely over the A1 by means of a bridge. The same instruction at the second sends me south into Wansford. The confidence I gain from being back on the route is knocked slightly when I note exit two is signed to Leicester. This proves a sufficient reminder that I am not nearly home, and I resolve to treat the remaining miles with a little more respect.

One minute after 6pm, I leave Wansford and Peterborough behind me, crossing the Nene into Cambridgeshire. The new county brings everything I expect of Tuscany, and nothing I expect of England. Fields of golden grain sigh under crystal clear skies. Bridges built in sienna shades. A palette of ochre and raw umber below the horizon, cobalt and Cerulean blues above.

The gently-rolling landscape has something of the battlefield about it. Although entirely idyllic in its contemporary setting, I know these are the same roads that nearly broke me on my way up. Sleeping riders dotted at the roadside provide gentle remembrance of the ongoing combat. Souls continue to be torn. Spirit, body and machines pushed to the absolute limit.

I follow a ridge through Sibson, discarded carcasses of aircraft providing the perverse advertising board that all rural airfields seem to favour. The sun casts long shadows but loses nothing of its warmth. Elton, Morbourne, peregrinate road dancing a hedge's breadth from Northamptonshire. The swells begin to build again as I plough through Great Gidding, Winwick, Old Weston.

Since rejoining the route I have been gradually catching and passing other riders, but on the approach to Catworth I find myself utterly scalped by the rapidly disappearing colours of a St Neots rider. Not happy with this, I give chase.

"No fair. You're local." I offer, catching his back wheel on the ascent.

"I've just finished my weekly training run!" he offers in defence, but doesn't slow up.

We push along neck and neck for the next few miles, happily trading conversation. Whilst neither of us is prepared to let the other edge in front, we're both happy to keep the effort level where we can still talk. Two foot to his starboard side, he has a clear view of the mechanics of the 'bent, and the carbon crankset is catching his eye. I want him to know I'm worthy of her.

"Gotta get her back to London tonight."

"Its too far, you won't be back until midnight" (I stay quiet. His timings are pretty optimistic).

"Did you ride up from London today?" he asks, re-evaluating my rig as a long distance speedster.

"No... I set off on Sunday" (he nods sagely),

"...but I have been to Edinburgh and back since."

He knows I roll faster than him on the descents but also that I'm speaking a lot less on the climbs. The varying gradients keep things competitive as we whistle through Kimbolton, drop under Stonely and charge through Staughton Highway. After a near flat out sprint into Hail Weston, he suddenly announces "This is my turn" and swings left. We keep our front wheels level until he is lost to sight behind houses.

In the dying sun I cross the A1 and the Great Ouse once again, coasting into St. Neots town centre. The road south from Eynesbury is shrouded in darkness but already I can detect the increasing trespass of city lights on the skies above. Knowing this may be my final chance to enjoy the Empyrean heavens, I spend the final seven miles to Gamlingay with my head tilted back, eyes lost in a sky that looks like talcum powder spilt on black velvet.

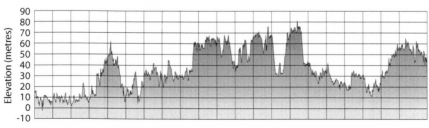

Thursday 2114hrs
Arrive Gamlingay Control.
4 days, 6 hours and 29 minutes in...
40 miles to go.

Entirely on autopilot, I follow the GPS into the car park, dismount, and join the line of riders at the controller's desk. 2.4 million years of evolution repurposed into a device for collecting brevet stamps. I have no faculty outside of progress. Clouded figures shift around me, chiaroscuro faces moving in soft focus across the plane. The shapes and noises are familiar, comforting. After a hot drink and some food, the resolution slowly begins to improve. I become aware of others as discrete identities, can zoom out enough to find myself in the scene.

Over time, slow revisions to the cast of our little enclave are enacted. The ensemble mask of enervation is maintained through a mechanic of inverse erosion. New players display absolute exhaustion. As each slowly becomes more purposed, he or she is replaced. I become aware that I am moving towards the head of the queue. I am seeing in colour. Soon I will remove myself. I prepare to leave, feeling like a free diver waiting to tumble from the skiff. Long deep breaths. Another world waiting below. A final dreamlike descent into darkness. I won't be coming back to this boat. I centre myself, focussing tightly on the tiny core that remains me. I can defend it against the perpetual eclipse of ongoing miles. I will make this.

Thursday 2214hrs
The final leg.

Giving up the warmth of the control, I exit left on the main road, south out of town. The lights of Gamlingay fade in my mirror as I begin to climb a wash of gentle risers. Emerging cyclists appear on the road behind me. Pinpricks of light, periodically clipped from view by the changing gradient.

No county wants to take ownership of the road. Over the next few miles the shires of Bedford and Cambridge volley us back and forth. At Guilden Morden, they finally combine efforts and spike us over the bump into Hertfordshire.

The passing towns are tiny. The fields are enormous. Always we swell. Up and down. Beyond Ashwell, the rhythm changes. Descents get shorter. The climbs begin to stretch out. Two steps up and one back, I slowly ascend to 140 metres. Crossing the A505, I can once again see flashes of red ahead of me. The shrill scarlet of LED lamps reflecting on wet gravel. From the patterns they're making, it looks to be a pretty big group. I push hard to catch them, closing as they slow for a sharp climb out of Rushden. Crossing Cromer Heath at midnight, we bring our own light to supplant the setting moon.

Travelling with twenty or more in the pack, our numbers are sufficient to block the increasingly small roads. Crank to crank, serried knees dance like oil derricks. A warm micro-climate of companionship keeps the drizzle and distance off my mind. I hang off the back of the group through the flatlands to Walkern, letting the hypnotic blink of rear lights guide me ever onward.

As we wind back into field-bordered lanes, I can detect the gradients sharpening. Strong riders at the front rise clearly above the group, pulling us through Benington, Burn's Green, Whempstead. Navigation points route-marked as towns seem to offer little more than occasional farmsteads. We start to snake. The surface quality drops away. Hedges close in.

The group responds by filtering into long streamers, rear markers slowing up as the formation re-shapes around us, extrusion pushing us back as chains extend ahead.

Potholes are called out. Navigation is automatic. With nothing in the foreground, my mind stumbles back to a conversation shared with Rich at Coxwold. Sat on a wall in a sun drenched car-park, he told me that almost every audax he'd been on featured an unnecessary climb. That he'd lost count of the number of times he'd seen a 'Church Hill' on a route that would otherwise be flat.

With 850 miles of my first audax now under the belt, I begin to further formalise these rules.

- If there's a choice of turns, and one goes up a hill, it's that one.

- If the road you're on has traffic, road markings or street lamps, and you pass a side road that doesn't, that's your turn.

- Ditto for flood defences, signage or any kind of maintenance plan.

- Extra points will be awarded if the road is unsuitable for vehicles.

- An optional bonus may be redeemable if the road is closed.

As it happens, the increased bunching up front is caused by exactly that. The pack filters to two streams, now passing either side of the red warning sign, and continuing along the broken surface without breaking pace. Unable to de-weight the bike, this becomes a notably technical section and I begin to lose ground. Although there is more room at the back, the increased rattling masks the fact that I've worn through another zip-tie and I soon throw the chain.

Stood in the dark, I am reminded that this is not a Friday Night Ride to the Coast. The 'leave no man behind' rule does not apply. The group ascend another hill, and are lost from sight. I perform a quick fix by torchlight, and set off in pursuit.

I don't catch them again until we hit the A602. The pack has slowed up, with some discussion about the route going forwards. There's been an accident up front. Rumour is an overseas rider traced his northbound GPS track the wrong way around a roundabout and came into contact with a vehicle. He's OK but there's a diversion in force whilst the scene is subjected to the necessary administration. Although we're less than 20 miles out of London, road choices are still slim pickings and we have no idea how far we may get sent off course.

Phone calls are made. Advice is sought. The routesheet wants to send us west, back through Hertford and Brickendon on rural tracks. Staying with the 602 will put us off-piste, but repair will be massively straightforward. There's no doubt we'll soon see the Great Cambridge Road and following that will deliver us via an urban dual carriageway straight to Lea Valley.

We opt to stay with the bigger road, riding the rollercoaster south through Bengeo Rural towards Ware and joining the slipway of the A10 at a major roundabout some two miles later.

Turning onto what I know is the road home, I gain a valued emotional lift. I can see the outlying 'burbs of London laid out beneath me and a ribbon of clear tarmac weaving me directly through it.

In another world, on a Sunday morning, I nervously wrote instructions for my wife on how to get to the start. I know the youth hostel is at the Cheshunt exit, barely two miles north from the M25. I have no idea how far up the A10 I am now, but I'm facing the right way and closing fast.

The A10

These then, are the final closing miles. I've done it. I've cycled from London to Edinburgh, and back. Just to be entirely safe, I ask the GPS to build me a route to the final control, and take some comfort from the resulting figures. 8.5 miles to the next instruction. Just under ten to Lea Valley. The backlit clock tells me its just gone 1am Friday. It'll all be over by 2.

The screen fades and won't light up again until it needs to flag my turn. Although I'm confident I won't miss my exit, I'm glad to have the GPS along. These roads aren't built at a human scale. The brutal authority of the tarmac subjugates the landscape, removing all indication of gradient, distance and time. Even the stars are lost to me, replaced by a flat grey light, the colour of orange juice mixed with cheap cola. There's no sense of progress and I keep my eyes firmly on the turning cranks, just to assure myself I'm still moving.

At the Rush Green exit I get my first real scare. Going slow on the concealed climb, I watch as the dotted line slowly unzips the safety of the hard shoulder. Cars slip by, left and right, at speeds in excess of 60mph. I'm too tired to be safe, and am not sure how long my confidence will hold out. I try to harness the passing lights to get interim measurements on the GPS screen, but am unable to pull out any figures. I'm still moving. Can't be more than six miles left. Close it. Finish.

The second exit drops away on a bluff above Stanstead St. Margarets. Another long drag, another long slip road opening. I'm losing speed, and beginning to get angry. Why are the exits always on a hill? Are things not hard enough? Oncoming vehicles spear my eyes with white hot blades of halogen and Xenon. The central reservation offers no protection to the recumbent eyeline. I can barely see.

Roadside signs approach in pairs, but resolve into single silhouettes as they come near. I can't hold focus. My cycle glasses are either damaged, dirty or fogged beyond any kind of use. I reach up to remove them, but my gloved hand makes contact with bare skin. I blink tight against the fog but dry tears scratch at my lids. I'm nearly done in. I can't pace myself. I need to know how much of this is left.

A new paranoia washes over me. Have I missed the turning? What if the GPS ran out of batteries before it could light up? I daren't reach forwards and try to revive it. In this traffic, its enough just to keep the bike straight. Sodium spills vandalise the cloud cover, but offer me no usable light. It can't be far. I must keep going.

My legs tell me that I'm climbing again as I approach the third exit, to Hoddesdon. Again my speed drops. Again I'm cast away from the protective solace of the kerb. As the gradient tops out, a series of lane closures send me further from its commission. Crossing the lane markings, I feel stranded in the middle of a motorway. Huge voids stretch between the raised lips of white paint to underline my laggard pace. This same surface will sound as a drumroll to cars coming over the rise behind me. No way to check my rear light is still on. I hope they are paying attention.

I filter through the roadworks, overhead arc lamps assuring me that the GPS is still alive. The numbers are still going down. I'm on track. It's hard going on roads like this. I remind myself I'm a Mouseketeer at heart. Big A-roads are supposed to be our declared route of preference. The end can't be more than two miles from here and I am not going to let this event simply trundle to a close. A descent to the Turnford exit gives me the impetus I need to get moving. I will sprint finish.

I redouble my efforts, pushing hard on the pedals, bringing my cadence up to a blur of shoelace and toe cap. I am bombing it. Soaring along. The wind is tearing at me, but this time I'm in control. It is my velocity and not the weather that brings the roar to my ears.

Even though I know I can't miss the turn, I'm still wondering whether that Garmin is working. I'm absolutely flying down the road but still the GPS hasn't chimed in. Come on. Give it some. Finish big. The little screen remains dark, but I know I've got to be almost there. It can only be a few seconds away. Full tilt boogie, I'm a recumbent missile.

Streetlamps rocket overhead, orange trails extending into stroboscopic blur of pure velocity. Houses and signs spring up. The North Cheshunt slip lane swings off and above me. As I roar under the roundabout, the GPS bursts into a brilliant display of information. I've cleared 38 miles since Gamlingay; my turning is a few hundred yards away; it's 1:42am and I'm closing at... 3.5mph?!

What frickin' gear am I in?

No time to worry now. I'm less than a couple of hundred feet from the crossroads. Shops on either side of the road tell me I'm in Cheshunt proper. I roll to a stop and gladly pull left off the A10. The GPS sends me along a short section of the official route but keeps me from the speedhumps. I can see Windmill Lane.

After days of carefully preserving the batteries, I can finally ease up and toggle through the Garmin's displays. The numbers mean nothing to me. One hundred and seven hours since I was last here. Eight hundred and seventy something miles, six of them on foot. Two days, eighteen hours and fifty three minutes on the bike. An average speed of eight point one five miles per hour throughout, raising to twelve point nine seven if you take off nine hours of sleep, all the eating, fettling and wandering around in a daze...

The bump of the level crossing jolts me back into the present. I tumble onto my feet as the front wheel hits the gravel car park of the Youth Hostel. The loose surface crunches underfoot as I trudge towards the bike stands, wheels scoring S-lines as I drag the 'bent beside me.

Parked up, I trace my way back to the double doors of the final control. The lights are on inside. I'm done.

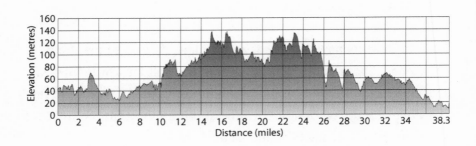

LEL DAY 6: FRIDAY

872 miles. Finished.
Photo: Evey Allsopp

Friday. 0151hrs
Lea Valley Youth Hostel. Finished.

On faltering legs I approach the desk and hand over my brevet card for its final stamp.

"Thank you. Well done." comes the response. I stand, dumbstruck as the controller files my card into a small drawer, exhaustion and propriety putting it firmly out of reach. I have carried this little piece of paper like a letter from a sweetheart. It has been within a foot of me all the way. Has accompanied me into each control. Has checked on me through long dark nights. My constant companion. My raison d'être.

He hands me a bag of trinkets in exchange and motions towards the continuing corridor. I'm still standing there twenty seconds later, when he says, "there are probably sofas upstairs."

Turns out this is the information I need to finally remove myself. I peer into the bag, pulling out a tiny golden key fob as I shuffle away. "London Edinburgh London. Rider 544/620."

With the dying bars of my phone battery I send a text to my wife to let her know I'm back safe. Lying in the dark upstairs, I manage to post to the forums, then, eyes fixed firmly on the little medal, descend below a glorious and impenetrable wall of sleep.

■ 31st Jul 2009, 02:05 — Top #54

arallsopp
Senior Member

Join Date: Aug 2008
Location: On a non-stop laptop pop strop.
Posts: 930

Is early. 😊

Got round in 107:06.

Hello.

Bed.

FNRttC videos 2009: Mar, Jun.

edit | quote

EPILOGUE

Tomsk was already safely round by the time I reached Lea Valley. GerryC, Greenbank and Xavier arrived at 0330hrs. Travelling with them for the final miles, Rimas completed his LEL within 114 hours. Deniece rolled in three hours later, inside the revised time limit and about an hour after sun up.

Brian made a brief appearance at the Lea Valley brevet desk during the night, before cycling on to the centre of London. By all accounts, he'd done the same thing at Edinburgh. "No point in doing that kind of distance when another 30 will seal it."

As I said, the man has issues.

Acknowledgements

Thanks go out to the participants, organisers, volunteers and communities that made LEL2009 possible. To Alex for having 'an idea', and the good folk of CycleChat and YACF for their support in making it real. To those around the web who kindly mailed me photographs after the event, and the patient encouragement of the CycleChat community as the narrative slowly came together. To Sue and Auntie Helen for bringing this to print, and my family for all the evenings donated to this project.

Lastly, my eternal thanks to The Mouseketeers. We never discovered the best road home, but somewhere in the hundreds of wrong miles ridden, found things that were far more important.

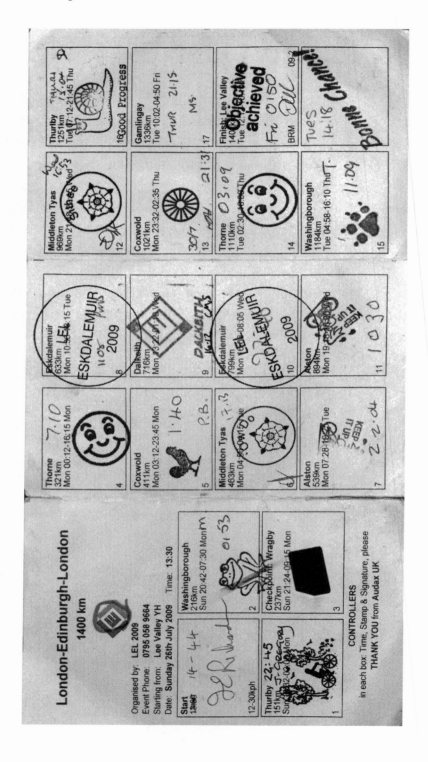

Printed in Great Britain
by Amazon.co.uk, Ltd.,
Marston Gate.